Where Authentic Leaders

This book demonstrates, complete with practical exercises, how to be successful in both your work and your personal life by becoming a truly authentic leader and empathic influencer. Above all, it shows you how to do this with the positive intention of successful, connected communication and through honouring the other person's perspective. The book is of particular value to managers and leaders who are very proficient in their areas of expertise and are looking for ways to improve team and personal performance further by developing their leadership and authentic influencing skills.

The book provides you with:

- Clear reasons why authentic leadership and empathic influencing will help in work and personal relationships.
- How to develop these influencing skills and remain authentic.
- The evidence, including the relevant neuroscience, as to why this is important.
- A 'how to' guide. If you are looking for some practical exercises to help develop authentic leadership, then you can go straight here.

Ruth Smith is Director of PM Management and is a highly experienced executive coach and facilitator. She has been coaching high-performing executives and board-level directors since 1990 and delivering her authentic leadership programmes for the past 10 years.

Where Authentic Leaders DARE

From Professional Competence to Inspiring Leadership

Ruth Smith

Routledge
Taylor & Francis Group

LONDON AND NEW YORK

First published 2020
by Routledge
2 Park Square, Milton Park, Abingdon, Oxon OX14 4RN

and by Routledge
52 Vanderbilt Avenue, New York, NY 10017

Routledge is an imprint of the Taylor & Francis Group, an informa business

British Library Cataloguing-in-Publication Data
A catalogue record for this book is available from the British Library

Library of Congress Cataloging-in-Publication Data
Names: Smith, Ruth, 1965– author.
Title: Where authentic leaders dare: from professional competence
to inspiring leadership / Ruth Smith.
Description: Abingdon, Oxon; New York, NY: Routledge, 2019. |
Includes bibliographical references and index.
Identifiers: LCCN 2019008088 | ISBN 9780367197667 (hardback) |
ISBN 9780367197674 (pbk.) | ISBN 9780429243158 (ebook)
Subjects: LCSH: Leadership.
Classification: LCC HD57.7 .S6537 2019 | DDC 658.4/092—dc23
LC record available at https://lccn.loc.gov/2019008088

ISBN: 978-0-367-19766-7 (hbk)
ISBN: 978-0-367-19767-4 (pbk)
ISBN: 978-0-429-24315-8 (ebk)

Typeset in Bembo
by codeMantra

Printed and bound by CPI Group (UK) Ltd, Croydon, CR0 4YY

To Rhian, Ben and Autumn
  'DARE to live authentically'

Contents

Preface

> Knowing others is intelligence.
> Knowing yourself is true wisdom.
> Mastering others is strength.
> Mastering yourself is true power.
>
> Lao Tzu

When I look around, I see all the different relationships that people have. There are the very personal relationships with your partner, children, brothers and sisters. There are the close relationships with your good friends. Then there are the relationships with your colleagues at work, be it your team, your peers or your boss. You also build a relationship of sorts with the people you only meet for a short time. In fact, unless you are a hermit or work alone in an office with no interaction, your life is made up of a series of relationships with others. The quality of these relationships can determine how successful you will be, how happy you are and crucially, how resilient you will be in the face of stress, change and uncertainty. Every connection with every person has the potential to be positive and rewarding, and yet so often the dialogue ends up being misinterpreted and frustrating. So how can you develop good-quality relationships that will lead to success, happiness and resilience? What can be done to develop deeply connected relationships that are rewarding, positive and characterised by profound trust? How can you realise your true potential with a focus on the relationships around you?

The aim of this book is to demonstrate, complete with practical exercises, how to be successful in both your work and your personal life by becoming a truly authentic leader and empathic influencer. Empathic influencing is the ability to understand your own and others' perspectives. To have exceptional self-awareness and deep knowledge of what you really think and feel. To be able to see something from others' perspectives almost as closely as they see it themselves. To be able to communicate, present information and interact at every level with an excellent appreciation of what will resonate with the other party. Above all, to do this with the positive intention of successful, connected communication and honouring the other person's perspective.

This book builds on my 20 years of experience as an executive coach who has worked with over 1500 senior leaders. It has been complemented by my research into authentic leadership and a review of leadership literature, as well as by my work with around 300 female leaders as they develop into authentic leading women. It has been further enhanced by my background of working with boards and senior teams, in addition to my own board-level experience. Consistently, I have found that people can hone their skills to become better leaders and family members just by having an astute understanding of how their communication 'lands' with others and by acting accordingly. Whilst some people may be excellent at managing upwards, they are less good at managing their teams and working with peers. They will find that 'spin' will only get them so far. The benefits of developing as authentic leaders with empathic influencing skills will be overwhelming in terms of achieving their own professional and personal success.

This book is for anyone who wants to be successful and recognises that, even with their experience and knowledge, something is missing that prevents them from achieving success and their personal best. Maybe you are starting to question whether your technical ability or knowledge is enough for you to realise your true potential. Perhaps you are working long hours and think there must be a better way. You may also feel that your children are growing up and you are missing out on this precious time. It is possible that you have seen other people who are less talented than you getting the promotions that you should have had.

How to use this book

The book consists of four parts and can be read either straight through or by picking the parts that are most relevant to you.

- The first part is about the reasons why authentic leadership and empathic influencing will help you at work and in your relationships.
- The second part addresses how you can develop these skills and remain authentic to who you are.
- The third part provides the rational evidence, including the relevant neuroscience, as to why all this is important and dispels the myth that we are rational as human beings. It also illustrates how authentic leadership and empathic influencing can be readily achieved with a better understanding of the human brain.
- The fourth part is a 'how to' guide. If you are looking for some practical exercises to help you develop, then go straight here.
- Finally, I offer some concluding thoughts about the real impact of developing these skills for the world.

Throughout the book I have used many examples to illustrate my points. Some are composites of a variety of people I have worked with. In others

I have simply changed the name, the gender (if not relevant to the example) and occasionally the sector. I have ensured that none of my clients are identifiable. I would like to add that I value all the experiences that my clients have shared and am very grateful for the time we have spent together and the mutual learning.

My life goal is to inspire, challenge and support people to create a sustainable and life-changing difference and lead truly authentic and happy lives. My experiences of working with many people suggest that there is a need for this book. I am hopeful that by sharing my thoughts in book form I can reach many more people, so that they can achieve success, authenticity and happiness.

Acknowledgements

I would like to thank a number of people who have supported me in the writing of this book.

Virginie Maisonneuve who initially encouraged me to write the book in the first place and gave me the confidence to do it. Carolyn Pearson for her ongoing support and encouragement and reading the drafts and making such positive recommendations. Deborah Larder-Shaw for her valuable input on the initial draft and also for being such a great work colleague. Elin Williams for her invaluable input on the first draft of the book. Talita Ferreira and Andrew Derrington for their review of the book proposal.

My brother, Professor Craig Smith, for his encouragement to get the book published. My brother, Roger, for his unconditional love and support, which enables me to be resilient in life and with the competing demands of writing a book, work and family.

For my eldest daughter, Rhian, who has helped in finalising the book with her more recent academic knowledge of referencing!

Anne-Marie Sonneveld, who, very patiently, has taken my poor stick men and other drawings and created some fun, memorable and thought-provoking illustrations.

Lynne Smith, who has worked with me for over 12 years and helped finalise the script for publishing. Thank you, Lynne, for your excellent attention to detail and your unwavering commitment and loyalty.

I could not have written this book without the rich experience of working with so many inspirational clients and I want to thank all of you for sharing your time and the mutual learning.

Part I

Why empathic influencing is important if you want to succeed as an authentic leader

1 Empathic influencing if used properly can be a powerful tool

Meet James. He is head of IT in a large organisation. James is exhausted and frustrated. He is working a 70-hour week and has been told he wouldn't be considered for promotion even if he put in 100 hours a week. His boss has informed him that technically he is brilliant – it's just that his peers don't warm to him or want to engage him with their IT issues. His team is effective and yet, when there is a crisis, they don't pull together or have the passion to resolve it.

James does not know what to do. He has no more to give. To further add to his frustration, his wife and children don't seem to understand. And when he thinks about it, he doesn't really know what they are all doing anyway. He is so tired that he just doesn't have the energy to enjoy life and spend time with those he loves. He can't even find the time and enthusiasm to go to school events or family gatherings. Is this what life is all about?

This is an all-too familiar scenario. Yet it can easily be changed by empathic influencing skills, which can put even people like James on a journey to authentic leadership. Empathic influencing is the most powerful way of getting on in organisations and in the world. Some might say it is the holy grail!

Imagine being able to read others' minds. The film *What Women Want* illustrates the power of telepathy in a comedy format. In the movie, Mel Gibson is able to read women's minds by hearing exactly what they are thinking (Goldsmith, 2001). Scary, I know, but just picture a world like that. If we knew what everyone was thinking, we would know exactly how to respond. What would that mean for us in our workplace, home and beyond? There would be no misinterpretation of information based on what we hope or (more likely) fear someone is thinking. No escalating anxiety with unhelpful hares running amok in your head. If this was a film, it would be a fantasy, yet it is a near possibility if we develop empathic influencing skills.

Four steps to becoming an empathic influencer

From working with hundreds of leaders, I have discovered that there are four levels to developing empathic influencing skills. All you have to do is DARE (Figure 1.1).

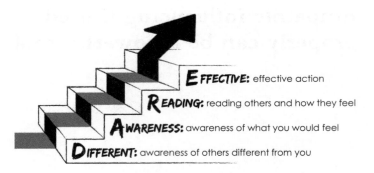

Figure 1.1 Four steps to empathic influencing.

1   Difference: realising that not everybody thinks/feels the same way as you do.
2   Awareness: of your own emotions and understanding of how you would feel in a given situation.
3   Reading others: recognising how the other person is not like you (e.g. they may be less confident) and really seeing the world through their eyes.
4   Effective action: communicating and connecting with the other person from an understanding of where they are coming from.

The majority of people operate from position 1. They are aware that other people are different, but simply accept that's the way it is and think no further about it.

People at stage 2 see the world mainly through their own eyes and experiences. What is positive is that they are working by the adage 'do unto others as you would have them do unto you'. However, this assumes that most others are like you. Quite often people operating at level 2 cannot understand why someone has reacted so badly to something they have said or done. They say, 'It wouldn't have upset me,' and are frequently surprised or even shocked by the reactions of others. We can also sometimes assume that others will be upset with some feedback, because we might be. In fact, they may be happy to receive it.

One of my clients, let's call him Rob, told me a story of innocently saying to a colleague that everyone knew she was in a relationship with one of the directors. The colleague didn't like to hear this and responded that she had worked very hard to achieve her current position. Rob wasn't questioning how she got there, but unfortunately that's what she heard and felt. The conversation escalated into a formal grievance and then mediation. Once again, when both read out their narrative of events and listened with the help of the mediator, the colleague misheard and even attributed comments to Rob that weren't actually made. The process didn't end well. My client couldn't see anything wrong with his remark from his own perspective. He would have been fine if it had been said to him. However, by looking at the colleague from her perspective he might have realised that his remarks could have been inflammatory to her. And he might not have lost his job (Figure 1.2).

Figure 1.2 Not everybody feels the same as you do.

Another good example came from Jane, an entrepreneur. She had developed a network of people who had supported her with developing her business. There was one man in particular who had been very helpful. She was a great advocate of this man and very appreciative of his advice and particularly his challenges. She would regularly refer to him as her business guru. One day she happened to bump into him whilst she was with a customer.

On this occasion, by her own admission, Jane was feeling somewhat 'giddy'. She has also confessed to having a very humorous, bantering relationship with the client in question. What followed was a huge error in judgement and she later described it as a 'massive failure of emotional intelligence'.

She introduced her respected guru with the words: "This is John, he is a complete tyrant". She then followed up with: "What he lacks in looks, he makes up for in brains". Ouch!

As you can imagine, he was less than impressed and responded the next day with an email. In his email he expressed his extreme upset with her, he couldn't believe that anyone could say such a thing and who did she think she was to say it. He felt that the comment was not only akin to sexual innuendo but even worse, a form of bullying. He went on to say that he had interpreted it that he was only worthy of conversation because he had the brainpower to help her so long as she didn't have to look at him. He finished by saying that he had never been so unimpressed with anyone in his life for being so shallow and that from here on he would no longer talk to her, respond to her emails and offer her any further support.

As you can imagine, in Jane's words, her momentary emotional intelligence failure resulted in irreversibly losing a relationship she truly valued.

People reach level 3 by really understanding how someone else sees the world. This is hard to achieve particularly in light of another old adage about 'walking a mile in someone else's moccasins'. Who really has time to do that? Furthermore, humans are inherently biased. We try not to be and yet research study after research study proves that we are. If we are really honest with ourselves, we know it. We hear some information and then make assumptions.

Doctor and writer, Danielle Ofri wrote in *The New York Times* in 2012 about a letter she had received from a professor whose first-year class had been assigned one of her essays, a story about a young woman in intensive care with a mysterious diagnosis. 'More than half the students,' the professor wrote, 'assumed that you were a man – despite your name. When asked why, many said that your writerly voice was unmistakably masculine: logical, confident, secure, sometimes sarcastic…and, above all, that you are an M.D.' (Ofri, 2012).

Yes, it can be difficult not to make erroneous assumptions about other people. But the good news is that it's not impossible, as we will see throughout this book.

Ultimately, it's all very well understanding how exactly someone differs from you; it's what you do with that awareness that counts – which is how you get to position 4. For example, if you're giving a presentation, does your audience like a logical, evidence-based argument or would it prefer an intuitive, emotionally engaging story? If you know what will make people happy or, conversely, trigger a negative emotional reaction, you will know how to connect and communicate with them.

Kevin, a managing director I once coached, was just about to start a new role. He wanted to show his boss, the group chief executive, that he was keen to get started. He sent an email requesting information as follows:

My exit from my current operation is on track. In view of preparing for my new role can you arrange and submit the following details for my review?

In itself, the request for information is positive. However, the tone in which it is expressed is negative. Words like 'submit' and 'review' could be construed as commands. In fact, it almost sounds as if the chief exec is working for Kevin, rather than vice versa. Add into the mix that this particular chief exec disliked anyone telling him what to do, and you can imagine that Kevin's new job didn't start well. By understanding his own tone and the person he was dealing with, Kevin could easily have ensured a positive reaction to his fundamentally positive action. If only he had written something like this instead:

My exit from my current operation is on track. To help me accelerate into my new role and deliver results, would it be possible for someone to send me the following information?

By developing empathic influencing, you can achieve a common understanding and connection. You will build a fantastic rapport with others and move along an accelerated path of mutual trust.

Empathic influencers demonstrate that they are listening and pay exquisite attention to other people. They hear not only what is being said in words but also, more importantly, what the person is saying with their body language and tone of voice. They can read other people and can sense their joy, frustration, uncertainty and (un)happiness. They know how to position ideas, issues and feedback so that they land with people.

I recall working with one team whose leader just couldn't understand why no one seemed to do what he asked. He complained that he would email them documents with all the information and instructions, explaining everything in full detail, yet nothing ever happened. The team members, on the other hand, complained that their manager wrote reams of information and instructions in his own lengthy and unique style. They all found it laborious and difficult to understand. Consequently, his emails remained unread and his instructions undone. As one team member articulated, the boss was throwing a ball of information but not in a way that he could catch it.

How empathic influencing fits with other aspects of emotional intelligence

There has been significant research demonstrating the crucial role of emotional intelligence (EI or, sometimes, emotional quotient [EQ]) in leadership. Take, for example, Daniel Goleman's classic *Harvard Business Review* article from 1998, 'What Makes a Leader?' (Goleman, 1998), or Andrea Ovans' overview published in the same journal in 2015, 'How Emotional Intelligence Became a Key Leadership Skill' (Ovans, 2015).

My own experiences support the research findings. Indeed, in numerous workshops, I have asked groups to tell me about a leader who has really inspired them. I get them to talk about what that leader did to make them want to give more and to make them feel positive and motivated. Then they have to write down the main behaviours and attributes of that leader. Without exception the lists consist of aspects of emotional intelligence and never mention technical skills or indeed intelligence quotient (IQ).

There are three main models for EI, the Goleman model, the Mayer–Salovey model and the Bar-On Model. Over the past twenty years I have extensively used the Bar-On Model developed by the psychologist, Reuven Bar-On. The Bar-On model of emotional-social intelligence has inter-related emotional and social competencies, skills and behaviours that influence how effective individuals are at understanding and expressing themselves, understanding others and relating with them, how they cope with daily demands, challenges and pressures. These have been further defined into fifteen factors that overall make up emotional intelligence (Bar-On, 2004). When applied to leaders, we can see that there are many facets to being an emotionally intelligent leader. See Figure 1.3.

My assertion and indeed coaching experience is that, whilst most of these facets are important in the leadership role, the focus needs to shift in favour

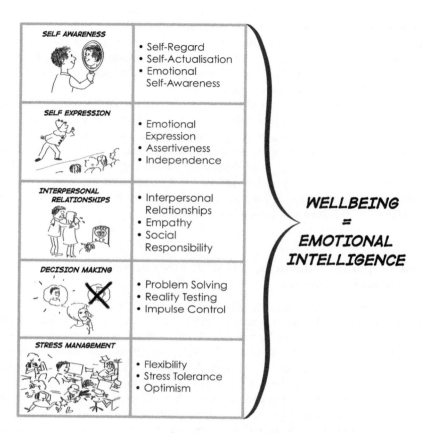

Figure 1.3 Based on Reuven Bar-On's 15 factors of emotional intelligence.

of empathy. This is particularly true for people who have a highly technical background, for example if they are in IT, finance or law.

A finance director (FD) from a financial services organisation, Sally, was considered to be technically the best FD her experienced CEO had ever come across. She really knew her stuff. Yet the other directors found her hard to work with and frequently came into conflict with her.

In appraisals, Sally was always rated highly on skills like 'understands and effectively manages resources' and 'demonstrates determination/drive to achieve objectives'. However, her lowest scores were for attributes such as 'demonstrates empathy for others' and 'shows sensitivity to the needs and feelings of others'.

In Sally's 360 evaluations there were often comments like the following:

- *"She needs to develop sensitivity to others".*
- *"She has no empathy for those who have to develop services for real people with reduced budgets".*

- "*Not totally convinced as to her level of sensitivity to more junior staff*".
- "*Sometimes cannot empathise with other points of view, often jumps to solution*".

Her team, whilst respecting her knowledge, felt undervalued and came to work to do a job. They were not prepared to give any more and this became apparent when the organisation hit a crisis.

As part of our coaching programme we undertook an emotional intelligence assessment. Sally's EI profile was typical of people in very technical roles. She scored very highly in problem solving, independence, self-regard and assertiveness, but ranked considerably lower on empathy, interpersonal relationships and, to a lesser extent emotional, self-awareness. This profile explained many of her problems with her colleagues.

Empathy can be developed

What I find endlessly fascinating about the people I coach is that, once the door to empathy, self-awareness and empathic influencing has been opened for them, they run through it – excited by this new world and the possibilities it offers. There is a sense of disappointment that they weren't introduced to this new world earlier in their careers. They can chart various issues, both personal and professional, that could have been prevented or resolved just by a greater awareness and skill in this area.

The even better news is that, yes, this awareness and skill can most definitely be developed, as psychologist Carol Dweck has shown with her work on the 'growth mindset' (Dweck, 2006). Of course, there are still some people who believe that empathy is a skill you are just born with, but this is clearly not the case. Certainly, my experience of working with hundreds of leaders suggests that an awareness of empathy and some clear strategies for developing it have yielded significant changes in their EI scores. Perhaps more importantly, what others say about them changes too.

Returning to Sally, our FD, twelve months after the coaching programme, the CEO described her as follows:

There has been a huge change in terms of the positive relationships that have been developed at board level, which in turn has enabled her to bring a huge change to the organisation. She has saved a lot of her own time and my time.

From Sally's own perspective she felt she had more inner confidence, was less defensive, had built some excellent relationships, read others well and felt more personally relaxed.

Downside of excessive empathy

However, it is also important to recognise that too much empathy is not necessarily helpful. As for many of the other emotional intelligence facets shown in Figure 1.3, it is important to achieve a balance. In fact, if you go too far, it can lead to other issues.

As I mentioned in my four-step model, a good starting point is to understand your own emotions fully. Great emotional self-awareness helps you to understand what you are feeling and thinking and how that might make you react in a given situation. Although that is not going to give you accurate and detailed information on others, it gives you a head start in thinking about what people like you might react to. Someone recently told me that she thought it was strange how she could be highly empathic but only with people who were just like her! What this person was describing was position 2 of our model. It's pretty easy to understand others if they are like us.

The greatest challenge to our empathy is those people who are most different to us – and yet that is precisely the challenge we need to rise to in today's diverse workplaces. What's more, all the research points to the fact that greater diversity brings greater innovation. The logical conclusion is that we need to move to position 3 and ultimately 4 to achieve innovation and competitiveness.

Another facet of EI that is almost as important – and often provides a counterbalance to excessive empathy – is high self-regard. Consider someone who is always thinking about how others might feel. So far so good, unless it also means they are always acting at their own expense. This may be appropriate on certain occasions, but it is not sustainable as a way of life.

In the corporate world, many people burn themselves out as they sacrifice what is important and necessary for them in favour of meeting other people's needs. They take on others' work when they can see that they are struggling. They say 'yes' to doing more hours. Then they go home and do all the household chores, because their partner is just so busy. I have seen this time and time again and it never ends well. One good reminder to such people is that we are told in an aircraft emergency to put our own oxygen mask on before helping others. This is also true for developing high empathy – we need to look after ourselves in order to help those around us more effectively (Figure 1.4).

Perhaps the most extreme scenario of low self-regard is domestic abuse, although it is highly complex from an emotional intelligence perspective. Working with a talented group of female police officers in the Public Protection Unit, I have learned that people suffering domestic abuse usually have high empathy. They understand that their abusers have 'had a difficult life' and that they 'don't mean to do it'. However, there is little acceptance of their own rights and even less belief that they don't deserve to be treated that way. They have low self-regard and even lower self-esteem. At the same time, the perpetrators have little empathy and perhaps are manipulators, which only helps to complete the vicious circle.

We see similar, if less extreme behaviour, from workplace bullies. The impact of low empathy can be catastrophic in any role that involves working with others. Not understanding others and responding to them insensitively can lead to miscommunication, misinterpretation and disastrous consequences. The following example highlights this.

Figure 1.4 Excessive empathy.

Susan, a managing director of a global business, took Tim, one of the board members, around one of the company's factories. She later described him as a bit of a "stuffed shirt with a plummy accent". At the end of the tour, Tim asked what the ethnic mix of the workforce was.

Susan was quite affronted by this. The factory employed a diverse range of employees and she felt that, just because they were not obviously from minorities, Tim had made some kind of judgement. She reacted angrily and in a condescending manner. Not a great career move.

Susan was jumping to conclusions about the comment. Her assumptions might have been true, or they might not. Either way, her reaction was based on only one possible truth. If she had explored the alternatives, she might have responded in a less hostile way.

Another illustration is played out in this real-life example. You can see the ping pong of a negative exchange culminating into a dialogue that has a negative downward spiral.

Edward is in a leadership team meeting with Jeffrey. Edward wants Jeffrey to reduce his budget by taking out headcount costs. Jeffrey knows that he is delivering an efficient service and suspects that Edward is only asking him so that he can further his own career.

Edward has many strengths. He is driven to succeed, likes to win and is good at seeing opportunities. He reacts strongly if he perceives that someone is threatening his status and he is made to feel 'less than they are'.

Jeffrey also has many strengths. He too likes to succeed. He is analytical, rational and always on top of his numbers. He reacts strongly to what he perceives as bullying, particularly from those he considers political: 'people who take decisions for their own self-advancement'.

In the meeting Edward observes that, as Jeffrey has the biggest headcount and they need to cut costs, he is the one who should find the savings. He says it in a confrontational and challenging tone. As he talks, he shoots a look over to the managing director.

Jeffrey responds with a perfectly rational explanation as to why that wouldn't work and comments on the naivety of the suggestion. His tone is condescending and patronising.

Jeffrey's response triggers a reaction at a very deep level. It reminds Edward of his father's constant comparisons of his poor school performance with that of his brother. He feels that he has been made to look stupid in front of his boss and his peers. He is highly sensitive to such public criticism and comes back fighting. He responds in an aggressive tone. In his desire to win he starts to construct a story that is not entirely factually accurate. He starts banging the table and finger-pointing.

Jeffrey is outraged by the inaccurate figures. He is even more outraged by this bully's threatening behaviour. He is not going to be the geek in the playground again, picked on just for knowing his stuff. He is going to show Edward exactly how wrong he is and he doesn't care how much he publicly humiliates him.

And so it goes on, with both Edward and Jeffrey spiralling into a vicious circle of negativity until the MD calls time.

After the meeting both resolve never to give the other anything. In fact, if they can damage each other in any way, then that is what they will do. Furthermore, when Jeffrey's department wants anything from Edward's department, he tells his people to put it at the bottom of their list. And vice versa.

This is just an everyday example that you probably see played out time and time again in meetings. It can so easily be prevented with just a little thought and a genuine desire to arrive in position 4.

Summary of key points

- Empathic influencing is the most powerful way of succeeding in organisations.
- There are four steps to developing empathic influencing skills:

  1 Different: realising that not everybody thinks/feels the same way as you do.
  2 Awareness of your own emotions and understanding of how you would feel in a given situation.
  3 Reading others and recognising how the other person is not like you (e.g. they may be less confident) and really seeing the world through their eyes.
  4 Effective action – communicating and connecting with the other person from an understanding of where they are coming from.

- Emotional intelligence is key, particularly greater empathy.

- High empathy needs to be balanced with other areas of emotional intelligence, particularly self-regard.
- Empathy is particularly relevant for highly technical roles, e.g. finance, law and IT.
- Empathic influencing can be easily developed once you know about it and how to achieve it.
- Lower empathy is at best a problem and at worst career limiting and catastrophic.

References

Bar-On, R. (2004). The Bar-On Emotional Quotient Inventory (EQ-i): Rationale, Description and Summary of Psychometric Properties. In G. Geher (Ed.), *Measuring Emotional Intelligence: Common Ground and Controversy.* Hauppauge, NY: Nova Science Publishers, pp. 115–145.

Dweck, C. (2006). *Mindset, How You Can Fulfil Your Potential.* New York: Random House.

Goldsmith, J., Yuspa, C. and Drake, D. (2001). *What Women Want.* Nancy Meyers. Icon Entertainment.

Goleman, D. (1998). What Makes a Leader. *Harvard Business Review*, vol. 76, pp. 82–91.

Ofri, D. (June 14, 2012). Assuming the Doctor's a He. *New York Times.*

Ovans, A. (April 28, 2015). How EI Became a Key Leadership Skill. *Harvard Business Review*, vol. 93 (digital article).

2 Technical skills become irrelevant at the top

When I look at senior leaders in organisations, what I notice is that – whilst their knowledge and technical skills have enabled them to progress so far – what defines their progression and continued success is their character and leadership style. Of the hundreds of leaders I have coached, from chief executives of large corporations to MDs of smaller businesses, their desire to enhance their effectiveness in their professional roles is never about plugging a knowledge gap; it's about becoming their personal best and an inspirational leader to others. As I mentioned in Chapter 1, when people talk about their experiences of great leaders, they don't mention knowledge or technical skills but how the leaders 'show up' (Figure 2.1).

When you are looking to hire someone do you offer the job to someone who had all the knowledge but seemed to have a poor attitude, difficult behaviour and problems in their relationships with others? Or would you employ someone who is keen to learn, motivated, works well with others and doesn't have all the knowledge… yet? When I ask senior leaders these questions, without reservation, they go for the second option. They believe

Figure 2.1 Technical skills become irrelevant at the top.

that knowledge is more easily gained than new attitudes, behaviours and interpersonal skills. This is becoming even more apparent with advances in technology and artificial intelligence.

Furthermore, at a certain level in organisations, knowledge and technical skills are a given. They are what qualified you to do the role in the first place. When you look to change your position, your technical skills may put your CV in the 'maybe' pile, but it is something else that gets you the interview and ultimately the job. This is also true when you go up for promotion, as we will illustrate in Chapter 4 with the PIE model. People who have successfully changed role invariably attribute their success to having a good network, interviewing well and being able to connect with others – all backed up by a history of delivery and performance.

Enjoying connecting and networking with others

Many people have a negative impression of networking, especially if they are not natural extroverts. They conjure up a picture of entering a room full of strangers, taking what feels like a big personal risk to approach someone (with the possibility of rejection) and then engaging in superficial small talk for a few hours until it seems OK to escape (Figure 2.2).

Whilst engaging in small talk with strangers might be a part of net-working, it only needs to be a minor element. If you consider some of the greatest things that have happened in your life, you may notice that they were the result of an introduction by a friend, colleague or family member. In essence, the best networking is with the people who know

Figure 2.2 The risk of networking.

you best and who will be an advocate for you. That's why it's so important to keep your connections and relationships alive. Clearly this relies on good communication, but it also rests on building great relationships in the first place.

When I work with clients on networking, I find that they initially express their dislike of it and then, when they think about it in the way I've just described, they recognise how important it has been in their lives to date. It also helps them to think about this when they are hiring people. If you are considering two candidates, both with the same qualifications, experience and technical skills, but one comes recommended by a colleague or friend, who are you most likely to recruit? When I ask leaders this question, they typically go for the person recommended by someone whose opinion they value. It makes sense – and it all makes even more sense with a little basic understanding of human psychology.

Our brains automatically categorise people as 'in group' or 'out group'. 'In group' people are usually similar to us, so we feel supported by and supportive of them. 'Out group' people are dissimilar to us, so there is an element of uncertainty and therefore a feeling of threat. At a deep level, we are constantly assessing who has or hasn't 'got our back'. Clearly then, when someone is recommended to us, it starts to promote the feeling that this person is more likely to be in our in-group and less of a threat to us. Recent research supports this even further. Biological factors such as gender, age and ethnicity, or social factors, such as profession, status, education or even preference for a sports team, can dictate whether we think of someone as in-group (one of 'us') rather than out-group (one of 'them'). This categorisation is the basis of social identity and comparison processes that yield biased perceptions of others (Molenbergh, 2013).

Obviously, this phenomenon has serious implications for diversity and the uphill struggle to minimise unconscious bias. However, it does demonstrate why our networks are so important.

A number of my clients have wanted support with networking and there are some great organisations that offer tools and techniques to help, such as checklists of what to talk about and tips for how to approach people. My experience suggests that the key is overcoming the hurdle of your own inner dialogue and reframing the whole networking experience.

One of my clients focused specifically on networking and in our initial conversation it was apparent that the main issue was his own self-confidence. This is his description:

Although I'd worked in customer-facing roles for a number of years, one of my biggest concerns was the way I dealt with both individuals and groups of people. I always took the view that people tolerated rather than accepted me. As a result, whenever I was in a large group, I would not feel confident enough to engage in conversation and would avoid speaking to people. My first goal was therefore to engage in conversation with a specific number of people at a seminar that we were hosting. It was a big departure from my comfort zone.

Although this was difficult at first, by the time I had broken the ice by introducing myself to one or two individuals, my confidence started to increase and I was then quite happy to engage in conversation. Although a very simple task, it made a great difference and I now actually enjoy interacting with people in that type of environment.

I was able to make a direct comparison between 'before and after', when we hosted a similar seminar three months later. On this occasion, I found that I was actively engaging in conversation with people I had not met or dealt with previously. I found that the more conversations I entered into, the more that my confidence grew.

In addition to my specific objectives, I also undertook an emotional quotient assessment. The test was useful in a number of ways. It helped me to confirm those areas where I could make improvements but also highlighted areas where I have particular strengths (such as empathy and independence). As a result, I focused my attention on those areas where I had recorded the lowest scores, but I was also able to reinforce the skills where my scores were higher.

I felt that my self-confidence increased significantly as I took opportunities to put my skills to test. It was, however, difficult to obtain an objective assessment of improvement. I therefore retook the assessment several months later, which confirmed that I had achieved improvements in a number of areas. This view was also supported by my line manager.

Be an exceptional interviewee with empathic influencing

While effective use of your network may get you in front of the decision-makers, you then have to wow them into offering you the role. This means you will need to be skilled at being interviewed. Once again there are numerous books and courses you can go on to prepare for an interview – and I would certainly recommend them. In addition, I'd suggest working on your empathic influencing, as it really comes to the fore in this situation. In a short interview you need to convince the people on the other side of the table that, not only do you have the right experience and qualifications for the role (your CV should have made that apparent in advance), but also you are a great person to employ – with behaviours and attitudes that will be an asset to the company. Although you can start to think through examples in advance of an interview, you will need to 'dance in the moment' with the interviewer, understanding what they value, building rapport and responding in a way that 'lands with them'. All this requires empathic influencing skills: the ability to really understand the other person, think about what's *really* behind the question, select relevant experiences to illustrate your response and then communicate your answer in a way that's effective for the interviewer.

There are a couple of 'old chestnuts' that are nearly always asked at interview:

1   What do you do well? Where could you do better?
2   Where do you see yourself in five years' time?

With question 1 the usual strategy is to think about what the role requires and then position both your strengths and areas for development in terms of them. For example, if the job advert requested 'someone who delivers results with pace', you will give evidence of how you have delivered results and then you might say that your weakness is impatience. This is all well and good and probably gives the interviewers what they want. However, if you have also researched the culture of the organisation and found that it prizes 'highly self-aware leaders who are mature and emotionally intelligent and resilient, looking to continuously improve', you may want to be more honest and reflective about your areas for improvement. The interviewer may rate you more highly if you dare to talk about a failure, your response to it and how that has shaped you. This would be particularly important if the culture of the organisation is one where 'failures can lead to innovation and creativity'.

Likewise, with question 2 you may talk about wanting to progress in the company and show your drive to succeed. Again though, if you really try to understand the organisation's objectives, you might find out that it wants a steady hand: someone to stay in the post for years. Conversely, some firms are happy for people to come, do a job and then leave to take up a better role elsewhere. A few may even reject you if they think that you aren't looking to move on in a few years' time.

As you can see with both examples, you need to really understand what's behind the question. It's not about being dishonest but about showing what you need to. Clearly, if that doesn't fit with what you want and is authentically you, then you need to make decisions about whether the organisation is right for you also. Simply understanding this simple fact will help you make better decisions about your career and life.

Increasingly for senior positions, the recruitment process gives your potential peers a chance to find out what they think of you and input into the recruitment decision. They may be involved in the interview or there may be a social gathering for you to attend. You definitely want the thumbs up from this audience and indeed you too will want to assess whether you could work with them. In a very short space of time you'll need to develop an accelerated relationship with your potential colleagues. This again is where your empathic influencing comes in.

What got you here won't always get you promoted

As people move up the organisation, it dawns on them that 'what got you here won't get you there'. At senior levels they need to employ new and different strategies. The most frequent false assumption is that people believe they will get on simply by working really hard and putting in long hours. As we will see in Chapter 4, performance is only one part of the equation for progress.

I once worked with a lawyer called Joe, who was very good at his job and had an excellent CV.

Most people in the firm assumed he would be next to make partner. But another colleague was also interviewed for the promotion. Joe's experience was far more impressive, but the colleague had done far more in terms of building relationships with the existing partners. Guess who got the promotion? I worked a lot with Joe on building his relationships with others, both in and out of his organisation. My main challenge was persuading him that this was as important as his lawyering – if not more so! (Figure 2.3).

Another time, I was coaching Diane, a commercial director. She had delivered unprecedented performance for her organisation. When the role of the MD became vacant, despite my client's superior performance, it was a colleague who had a long-standing

Figure 2.3 Technical brilliance vs. what the audience wants.

relationship with the chief executive who got the job. Based purely on logic, it didn't seem the right decision – and yet I have seen Diane's scenario repeated time and time again in organisations. If you want to progress, you need to see your role as more than just your performance.

Sometimes my clients have been able to deploy simple strategies to help them engage with their networks. For example, some have kept a spreadsheet of their contacts, complete with partners' and children's names, hobbies and recent holidays. They have the database to hand so they can refer to it when they speak to people on the phone. Just think what you might feel when someone you have only met a few times appears to remember such information. You would almost certainly feel valued. So starts the development of a deeply connected relationship.

It's easy enough to conclude that knowledge, experience and technical skills are the not the critical elements for progressing in an organisation. But what *is* required to reach at senior management or board level in an organisation?

It seems that an increasing amount of attention is focused on performance with others in a team or meeting setting. Take, for example, the Financial Reporting Council's summary of requirements for evaluating boards (see Guidance on Board Effectiveness – FRC July 2018):

- The mix of skills, experience, knowledge and diversity on the board, in the context of delivering the strategy with the challenges and opportunities and risks facing the company.
- Clarity of, and leadership given to, the purpose, direction and values of the company.
- Succession and development plans.
- How the board works together as a unit, and the tone set by the Chairman and the CEO.
- Key board relationships, particularly Chairman/CEO, Chairman/Senior Independent Director, Chairman/Company Secretary and Executive/Non-Executive.
- Effectiveness of individual Non-Executive and Executive Directors.
- Clarity of the Senior Independent Directors' role.
- Effectiveness of board committees, and how they are connected with the main board.
- Quality of the general information provided on the company and its performance.
- Quality and timeliness of papers and presentations to the board.
- Quality of discussions around individual proposals allowing sufficient time.
- Process the Chairman uses to ensure sufficient debate for major decisions or contentious issues.
- Effectiveness of the Secretariat.

- Clarity of the decision processes and authorities; reflecting and drawing on key decisions made over the year.
- Processes for identifying and reviewing risks; and
- How the board communicates with, and listens and responds to, shareholders and other stakeholders (FRC, 2018).

As you can see, the vast majority of these criteria centre on how you 'show up' at meetings. How do you lead? Can you work effectively in the team? Can you communicate? Can you challenge others? Whilst it is a given that you know your subject area, what counts is how this is played out in the boardroom.

Exceptional team performance where 2+2 = 10

The board of directors is just one of many contexts where companies emphasise good team working. Organisations can see that high-performing teams have significantly higher collective outputs than a bunch of high-performing individuals working independently. The results are not down to individual team members' technical skills but how they come together and create something more than they would on their own. A good team consistently produces more than the sum of its individual parts.

There are numerous characteristics shared by most high-performing teams. In a 2012 *Harvard Business Review* article, 'The New Science of Building Great Teams', Alex Pentland revealed that in successful teams:

- Everyone on the team talks and listens in equal measure, keeping contributions short and sweet.
- Members face one another and their conversations and gestures are energetic.
- Members connect directly with one another not just with the team leader.
- Members carry on back-channel or side conversations within the team.
- Members periodically break, go exploring outside the team and bring information back (Pentland, 2012).

Most recently Google's Project Aristotle, which looked at 180 teams from throughout the company, concluded that 'there was nothing showing that a mix of specific personality types of skills or backgrounds explained the difference in performance between teams'. It turns out that the two factors that made the biggest difference were:

- In good teams, members spoke in roughly the same proportion, i.e. there was 'conversational turn taking'.
- Good teams all had high 'social sensitivity', i.e. they were skilled at intuiting how others felt based on their tone of voice, their expressions and other non-verbal cues (Duhigg, 2016).

These two conditions create the psychological safety and trust that provide the basis for healthy dialogue. More specifically, the 'social sensitivity' that Google identifies is almost exactly what I described in stage 3 of my DARE model of empathic influencing in Chapter 1: reading others and how they feel, recognising that the other person is not necessarily like you.

When working with a senior team, I am always keen to understand what drives people's behaviour and how that plays out in a team setting. For example, for people in the team who get satisfaction from winning the content of the discussion becomes less important than carrying the argument. Meanwhile, others who are concerned with their own status will favour decisions that make them look important.

It is essential to look for the team dynamics. What will help the individual members achieve their objectives? And what might hinder them? Conflicting emotional drivers can derail a team either from achieving its objectives or simply create friction that slows them down.

A few years back, I worked with a commercial team of nine people in a global manufacturing and distribution organisation. The company had devised a bold new strategy to overhaul its production and processes and sourcing of materials. The overall aim was to reduce costs significantly. But the commercial team was not working effectively. It was not cohesive, there was a lot of infighting and the nine individuals needed to pull together if they were going to deliver the radical new strategy.

Each of the team members complained that there was little in the way of mutual support – and this was borne out by the behaviour I initially observed. None of them liked to express emotions – and there was a double whammy, as most of the nine were low in empathy and self-awareness. In other words, they were hopeless at reading the most obvious emotions, whether their own or their colleagues'. They were all quite insular, uncomfortable needing others and happier succeeding on their own. Nevertheless, a few of them liked to be in charge, so there had been power struggles. To make matters worse, the official team leader had a highly autocratic style of making decisions.

On the plus side, it was a highly analytical and rational group of people, which included a number of trained negotiators. It was a classic case of high rationality and low expression of emotion, which makes for excellent individual performance but tends to be a hindrance in a team setting. The other good news is that they were also highly flexible and willing to adapt their beliefs and values according to the situation.

My first task was to hold up a mirror that focussed the team on its motivations. By considering why they behaved as they did, everyone could see how they needed to adapt to raise their performance and become the best team in the company (one of their main drivers). Next, we worked together on developing self-awareness and empathic influencing to help them read themselves and others better. A year later, an internal survey revealed that they were the most effective team in the organisation – and their success cascaded down to the people who worked for them. As for the radical new strategy, it is delivering results for the company across the globe.

The moral of the story is that each team has its own unique profile and the individual emotional drivers tend to be reflected in the behaviours and success of the group.

Around the same time, I was working with another very different team. They were senior leaders in a large public-sector organisation, responsible for changing the way it worked both with the public and internally. They had to move from bureaucratic accountability to democratic accountability, away from high 'command and control' to an environment where staff were empowered. Their other goal was to change public perception of their service to include accountability, accessibility and transparency.

In this case, it was apparent that the group was very driven to build close connections with individuals and other teams. They were highly empathic people and open to expressing their feelings both verbally and non-verbally. Furthermore, they were highly motivated to 'do the right thing' and had a clear purpose and strong values. They were less keen on operational detail and had a direct rather than an opportunistic approach. Working with this team was about understanding and identifying their key strengths individually and collectively so that they could leverage them to enable the achievement of the goals above. By understanding their individual motivations and how that translated into their own personal purpose, sharing that with their colleagues enabled them to develop an inspiring purpose for the organisation and, in turn the people they led.

Although not measured, we can already start to see that this second team has a number of facets required of authentic leaders. Their drivers were exactly what was needed for their individual roles and their challenge and vision for the organisation. If you tried to put the people in the first team in this role or vice versa the outcomes would probably be disastrous. In both of these cases we can see that it is not about their knowledge or technical skill that would drive success it is about how they are driven as individuals. What would be interesting is who would be most successful or least disastrous. My sense is that it is the second team that would be able to adapt with a more authentic leadership style and drive results through the people with empathic influencing. Whilst both team of leaders progressed to being authentic leading teams, it was easier and faster for the second team. Great leadership can take a bus in any direction with the right driver. Authentic leadership is considered to be the 'gold standard' for great leadership. In the next chapter, we will look at what great leadership is all about.

Summary of key points

- Knowledge and technical skills will get you considered for promotion but you need empathic influencing to get the job.
- Networking skills is best developed with empathic influencing.
- You are more likely to be hired by someone in your network and vice versa.
- Empathic influencing will help you in a job interview by enabling you to understand what is really behind a question and to develop positive relationships with potential colleagues.
- Building relationships can be more important than past performance when going for promotion.

- Performance at board level is about much more than knowing your subject area.
- High-performing teams are characterised more by their behaviour with each other than by excellent knowledge and technical skills.
- It is important to understand what drives and motivates a team and how that corresponds to the goals of that team.

References

Duhigg, C. (2016). What Google Learned from Its Quest to Build the Perfect Team. *New York Times*, February 25.

Financial Reporting Council Ltd. (2018). Guidance on Board Effectiveness, p. 29, July 16, 2018. Accessed: October 12, 2018. www.frc.org.uk.

Molenbergh, P. (2013, September). The Neuroscience of In-group Bias. *Neuroscience and Biobehavioural Reviews*, vol. 37, no. 8, pp. 1530–1536.

Pentland, A. (2012). The New Science of Building Great Team. *Harvard Business Review*, vol. 90, pp. 3–11.

3 Leadership

As you progress through an organisation you will be taking on leadership roles, where the ability to inspire and motivate others becomes a key requirement. So often organisations promote the best technical person only to find that it just doesn't work either for the individual or for the organisation. When 'experts' become leaders they are often ineffective – and sometimes total failures.

Scott had been with his company for eight years. He had joined as a graduate trainee in sales and had considerable success. He had then moved into field sales and from there on to account management. In each of these roles he had increased revenues from new and existing clients. He had exceeded all of his targets given and gained a 'golden boy' reputation within the company.

Scott was ambitious and the company wanted to keep him, not least because of his performance but also because of the threat of losing the sales to a competitor, should he walk. The next natural step was to lead the field sales team reporting into the sales and marketing director. And at the age of 30, Scott was promoted to this role.

The next nine months were the worst of Scott's whole career to date. Field sales fell by 25% whilst those of the competition rose. The team's previous star performers were feeling so under-valued, demotivated and frustrated that they were looking at leaving. Scott himself had gone from 'hero to zero' in the eyes of the organisation. His bosses were deeply concerned about the sales performance and the feedback about his leadership or, rather, lack of leadership. They heard that he was not setting any direction for the sales force and they felt rudderless. The team had no idea what the sales strategy was and just continued doing what they thought was best. There was no discussion of how they were performing and no coaching to help them do better. In fact, it was clear that Scott would avoid any difficult conversations. This particularly demotivated the high performers as they felt that they were carrying the low achievers.

Scott was deeply unhappy. He had been thrilled at his promotion and, although it brought the title and expectation of leadership, he didn't really understand what that meant. He thought it was just a bigger sales job. He hadn't appreciated that his role was now to enhance the performance of others. He wasn't even sure if that was what he wanted. He liked the status but, as he was no longer on commission, it also meant a big reduction in income. And now that the sales team wasn't performing, it didn't look as if he was going to get his bonus either.

Scott was in sales, but I've seen the same scenario played out by lawyers, IT professionals, engineers, academics, accountants and many other technical specialists suddenly catapulted into a leadership role that they don't fully understand.

Exceptional leadership

The skills at the leadership level, where you are required to motivate, inspire and coach others, are very different from expertise in one particular area. In fact, your technical skills become secondary to other attributes, as I will illustrate throughout this chapter.

In Chapter 1, I described the exercise that I frequently use, asking people to describe a leader who has inspired them and made them want to give their best. Here's my consolidated list of responses:

- Trusted me.
- Believed in the team.
- Was confident of success.
- Was willing to invest time and effort in us.
- Allowed me to make mistakes but learn from them.
- Empathised.
- Connected with people.
- Appointed the right people at right time.
- Gave us head space.
- Was always positive.
- Set us free (but with safety net).
- Delegated but didn't abdicate responsibility.
- Mentored and coached people.
- Inspired the team.
- Had a clear vision.
- Did the right thing.

As you can see, technical skills don't appear at all.

There are thousands of articles on what makes a great leader and yet it's hard to pigeonhole most great leaders. Nelson Mandela was very different from Richard Branson, for example. When I look at the research, history books and my own experience of working with hundreds of leaders who seem to get the best from their people, I can only echo the findings that it's the truly *authentic* leaders who set the gold standard. Great leadership is authentic leadership, which I'll attempt to explain in the course of this chapter.

Proven benefits of authentic leadership

With all the dramatic changes in the world today, people are calling out for more authenticity from the people who lead them. Whilst we see this as to how people vote on crucial issues, we can also see this by the Edelman trust barometer. Edelman undertakes an annual survey with populations throughout the world and develops the trust barometer. Over the past few years the barometer has shown people's trust in crisis with societal institutions, media and leaders. What is interesting is that in 2019 there has been a shift towards greater trust to more local (and therefore controllable) sources, specifically their employer. Clearly, people are looking for the trusting relationship an authentic leader will offer.

There is a noticeable shift throughout the world and people are voting for something different. Regardless of politics, it is clear that there is a groundswell for a different kind of leadership. Although I would argue that some of the people who have got into power are not authentic leaders, they were elected because they promised what people needed and crucially voters felt listened to.

Being an authentic leader is hugely beneficial not only to the leaders themselves but also to their followers. A review by Datta (2015), when assessing the effectiveness of authentic leadership, showed in his article that authentic leadership

- increased trust in management and positively affects group performance with increased sales (Clapp–Smith, Vogelgesang and Avey, 2009);
- increased trust in the leader and work engagement (Hassan and Ahmed, 2011);
- was the single biggest predictor of employee job satisfaction, organisational commitment and work happiness (Jensen and Luthans, 2006);
- had a negative direct effect on workplace bullying and emotional exhaustion and a positive effect on job satisfaction (Laschinger, Wong and Grau, 2012);
- is positively related to follower job performance (Peterson et al., 2012);
- led to followers' satisfaction with supervisor, organisational commitment and extra effort as well as perceived team effectiveness (Peus et al., 2012);
- had a positive relationship with followers' psychological capital, partially mediated by positive work climate and a significant moderating effect from gender (Wooley, Casa and Levy, 2011, Datta, 2015).

From my own literature review, these are further supported with many other pieces of research demonstrating the positive impact of authentic leaders on their teams, organisations and results.

In addition, there are even some studies – particularly relevant in today's world – to suggest that authentic leaders make more ethical decisions. It would also seem that authentic leaders are happier and live better balanced lives than non-authentic leaders.

What exactly is and isn't authentic leadership?

So, what exactly do we mean by authentic leadership? If we break the term down into its two component parts, we can define it as follows:

Authentic means genuine, real and true – not copied or false. Your *authentic self* is based on the tenet 'to thine own self be true'. It's the 'you' that can be found at your core.

Leadership has many definitions, but common to most of them is the idea of the behaviour of an individual directing the activities of others in the achievement of a shared goal.

When running leadership programmes, I am frequently asked questions like this:

> One of our leaders is abrupt and rude. When we challenge him, he just says, 'Well that's just the way I am.' Is that what you're suggesting? Should we be true to ourselves, however negative our behaviour might be?

While the abruptness and rudeness may well be authentic, think about the combination of the words 'authentic' and 'leadership'. It's important to distinguish between authenticity, leadership and authentic leadership.

So, my response to the question above is two-fold. First, what is the truly authentic person? And second, where is the leadership component? An authentic leader has a responsibility not only to the people he or she is leading but also, as a responsible citizen, in all of his or her relationships, both personal and professional.

What really is the true person? The authentic self is what we are without the expectations, fears or limitations imposed on us, either by ourselves or by others. Finding your authentic self is a radical form of self-awareness, which involves understanding who you are at your core and what really drives you. It's like peeling away the layers of an onion. Are you really rude and abrupt deep down or have you developed this behaviour to deal with your inner perceptions or indeed demons? Are you possibly covering up for your own insecurities? Or are you maybe exhibiting 'imposter syndrome', that is, not seeing or internalising your own accomplishments accurately and having a persistent fear of being exposed as a 'fraud'? There are all kinds of reasons why people's behaviour does not necessarily reflect their authentic selves.

Now let's take the leadership component. Leaders have a responsibility to get the best from others to enable the achievement of some goal. How does being rude and abrupt (or any other behaviour that has a negative impact on others) achieve that?

So, all in all, my final answer to the question is: no. Being an authentic leader does not mean that you can freely engage in bad or destructive behaviour.

As an authentic leader, your values and character will remain constant and strong. If we use a tree analogy, they are your roots. The extent to which you will show and disclose all of your values and character will depend upon your environment. If your environment is supportive and positive (or sunny; see Figure 3.1), you may show a lot of yourself. However, if your environment is cold and hard, you may choose to be selective about what you disclose. You

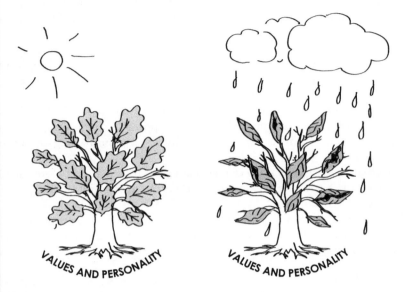

Figure 3.1 What you choose to show will be determined by your environment.

are no less authentic, you are just reading your environment and making choices about your best response to it. Clearly, as with the tree analogy, it is not sustainable to be in a cold, harsh environment indefinitely.

Defining authentic leadership

Authentic leadership is a fairly new area in academic research. I think that the best definition comes from the American academic, Bruce Avolio:

> Authentic Leaders are deeply aware of how they think and behave and are perceived by others as being aware of their own and others' values/moral perspectives, knowledge and strengths; aware of the context in which they operate; and who are confident, hopeful, optimistic, resilient and of high moral character.
>
> (Avolio, 2004)

Most of the research has identified three key themes:

- Authentic leadership is informed by the 'true self'.
- Self-awareness is a key component of authenticity.
- Authentic leadership is strongly connected with moral leadership.

In terms of defining and further understanding the construct, authentic leadership, Walumbwa and associates (2008) reviewed the literature, interviewed relevant content experts and developed a measure of authentic leadership. Their research identified four components for authentic leadership:

Self-awareness – an understanding of one's strengths and weaknesses and the multifaceted nature of the self; this includes developing an insight into the self, through exposure to others and being aware of one's impact on others.

Internalised moral perspective – self-regulation that is based on internalised moral values (as opposed to those imposed by the group, organisation or society); this is expressed in ethical decision making and ethical behaviour.

Balanced processing – an objective evaluation of information before making a decision, including encouraging others to question or challenge one's values.

Relational transparency – being true to one's values and expressing this to others; this involves the open sharing of information about one's thoughts and feelings.

Based on these components, there's also a questionnaire to determine your authentic leadership score, the ALQ (go to www.mindgarden.com for details) (Walumbwa et al., 2008; Avolio et al., 2009).

Additionally, whilst these four factors are the basis for authentic leadership, there are other factors that influence authentic leadership (Luthans and Avolio, 2003). These other factors include positive psychological attributes, specifically, confidence, hope, optimism and resilience; moral reasoning, i.e. making ethical decisions on issues of right or wrong; and transformational life events that shape a leader's life. They can be both positive events such as having a child or negative events, for example losing a loved one (see Figure 3.2).

I think this model is useful to provoke thought and certainly for academic research. However, my experience of coaching hundreds of leaders is that to embark on the journey of self-development, you need a simpler and more practical model. Based on my coaching experience and others' research, I've created my own authentic leadership model, as shown in Figure 3.3.

In brief, the four components are as follows:

Living life with purpose and passion means understanding what you are good at and what you love doing – and ensuring that you are living in service of that both at work and at home. It is about thinking and feeling that your work is a 'calling'. A couple of research projects have demonstrated that those who feel their work is a calling have greater life and work satisfaction, less absenteeism, better results, better self-worth and zest for life (Peterson et al., 2009; Wrzesniewski et al., 2010). The Austrian neurologist and psychiatrist, Victor Frankl, even showed that people who understand their 'why' are more resilient and were more likely to be Holocaust survivors (Frankl, 2004).

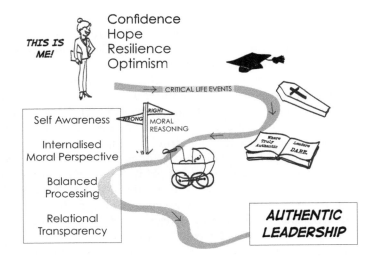

Figure 3.2 Authentic leadership journey based on Luthans and Avolio (2003), and Gardner et al. (2005).

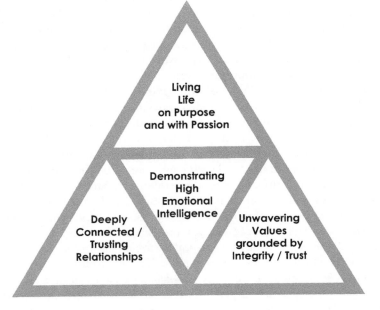

Figure 3.3 Authentic leadership model.

Unwavering values grounded by integrity and trust means being clear about what your values are and what you stand for. Neuroscience confirms the business research: leaders who demonstrate high integrity and trust will inspire people to want to follow; and those with solid values provide consistency and certainty of behaviour through both good and bad times.

Deeply connected relationships mean connecting at a deep level with your followers. It's about seeing people as people and seeking to understand them and their motivations more profoundly. One way to think of this is to consider who in your life you have a deeply connected relationship with. Perhaps it's your partner or your best friend. Then think through the characteristics of the relationship and what that means to you/them. If you're like most people, you'll probably identify honesty and trust. This kind of rapport means that you can sometimes get feedback that's difficult to hear, but because you know the intention is positive, you willingly accept it and learn from it. Indeed, you may even be grateful for the new perspective! Furthermore, you feel valued, appreciated and want to give your very best to that relationship. Now imagine having these connected relationships, with the benefits described above, and what that could mean in the context of the workplace – for you, your boss, your team and your organisation?

Demonstrating high emotional intelligence is the enabler for the other three elements of the model. If we consider Reuven Bar-On's factors for emotional intelligence (shown in Chapter 1), there is an overlap with all of his factors and the three elements of the model. Particularly we can see that people with high self-actualisation, self-regard, optimism and emotional self-awareness will strongly influence people living a life on purpose and with passion. Unwavering values grounded by integrity and trust will be impacted by social responsibility, emotional expression and assertiveness. Empathy, interpersonal relationships emotional expression and impulse control strongly influence deeply connected relationships (Bar-On, 2004).

Clearly this simple, practical model draws on the more academic model we saw earlier. But it also focuses on two additional and crucial elements: purpose and empathy. It seems that you could score highly on the theoretical model and yet have no clear view of your purpose. In my experience, authentic leaders appear to have a clear life purpose – and this purpose becomes highly engaging and infectious to their followers. Similarly, the academic model's focus on self-awareness neglects empathy and empathic influencing, both of which are essential to the 'leadership' aspect of 'authentic leadership', even if they aren't strictly necessary for authenticity.

In 2015, Professor Herminia Ibarra, one of the world's top leadership experts. wrote an article for Harvard Business Review *called 'The Authenticity Paradox' (Ibarra, 2015). In it, she described a leader called Cynthia, who had taken on a huge new role with a tenfold increase in direct reports. Cynthia felt uncertain and 'shaky' about the bigger responsibility and, as a transparent, collaborative leader, she expressed her fears to her new employees by admitting that she was scared and needed their help. This didn't land well, as she lost credibility with her direct reports, who wanted someone confident to take charge. To my eyes, this is a clear-cut situation. Cynthia failed as a leader of people, not as an authentic person. If she had used empathic influencing skills, she would have succeeded. First, she would have had enough self-awareness to know how she was feeling. Second, she would have thought about what would happen if she expressed what she was feeling to others. She might initially have assumed – at level 2 of the DARE model (see Chapter 1) – that she would be fine with a boss who disclosed such doubts, but then, if she moved to level 3, she would realise that many members of her new team might feel differently. She would then step up to level 4 and into their shoes. There she would see that they might be scared and want guidance, but most of all that they needed to know their leader is not fazed by the challenge in hand. Being an authentic leader is not about baring your soul and disclosing feeling with no responsibility for how that might land with others. There may be a good time for self-disclosure to build trust and intimacy, but Cynthia certainly didn't find it (Ibarra, 2015).*

Empathic influencing is essential for authentic leaders

I have extensively coached over 1500 leaders from a wide range of public and private sector organisations. There have been chief execs, MDs, finance directors, IT directors, COOs, sales directors, managing partners at law firms, and deans and pro vice chancellors from universities. They have all been successful and wanted to get even better. And in many of these cases, the missing link to being the best they could be was empathy and empathic influencing. I have come to believe that it is essential for a leader, particularly a leader who is motivated to achieve great results.

The big surprise to me is that so few people understand the importance of empathy to good leadership. In 2012, two academics in California, Svetlana Holt and Joan Marques published some research from a three-year study of business graduates and MBA students. The future leaders in their sample consistently rated empathy as the least important skill for leadership from a choice of ten (see Figure 3.4) (Holt and Marques, 2012).

Furthermore, when the two researchers looked at what was happening in corporations, there seemed to be a predominance of the senior leaders exhibiting signs of narcissism and psychopathy. This is just one of many recent studies on the psychopathic nature of leaders. Although difficult to prove, it has been estimated that approximately 3% of the leadership population have psychopathic qualities compared to 1% in the general population. As author Victor Lipman commented in a 2013 article in *Forbes* magazine:

The hallmarks of the psychopathic personality involve egocentric, grandiose behaviour, completely lacking empathy and conscience. Additionally, psychopaths may be charismatic, charming, and adept at manipulating one-on-one interactions. In a corporation, one's ability to advance is determined in large measure by a person's ability to favourably impress his or her direct manager. Unfortunately, certain of these psychopathic qualities – in particular charm, charisma, grandiosity (which can be mistaken for vision or confidence) and the ability to 'perform' convincingly in one-on-one settings – are also qualities that can help one get ahead in the business world. (Lipman, 2013) (Figure 3.5).

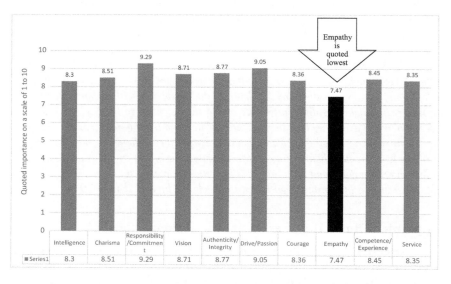

Figure 3.4 Importance of Leadership Qualities (Holt and Marques, 2012).

Reprinted by permission from Springer Nature: Journal of Business Ethics. Empathy In Leadership: Appropriate Or Misplaced? An Empirical Study On A Topic That Is Asking For Attention. Holt, S. and Marques, J., (2012).

Figure 3.5 Narcissistic and psychopathic leaders.

The good news is that, whilst reality appears to be lagging behind, there appears to be a groundswell of business gurus, researchers and crucially employees promoting the increasing need for empathic leaders. For example, some researchers (Gentry et al., 2017) at the Center for Creative Leadership, a specialist executive education provider, looked at a sample of over 6,700 leaders from thirty-eight countries. Here's what they found:

> *Our results reveal that empathy is positively related to job performance. Managers who show more empathy toward direct reports are viewed as better performers in their job by their bosses. The findings were consistent across the sample: empathic emotion as rated from the leader's subordinates positively predicts job performance ratings from the leader's boss.*

> (Gentry et al., 2007)

Global assessment specialists, the Management Research Group, also found in 2017 that the top-performing 5% of leaders had significantly more empathy than those in the lowest-achieving 5%. (see Figure 3.6) (MRG, 2017).

Furthermore, they found that those managers who were most likely to derail were the least likely to be empathic or self-aware.

Although I had my own intuitions and a huge pile of academic research suggesting that empathic influencing should be a key element of authentic leadership, I decided to test this further. I set out to compare the authentic leadership scores of my clients with their assessments for

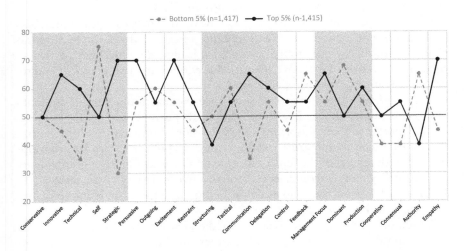

Figure 3.6 Comparison of the top 5% with the bottom 5% on the Leadership Effectiveness Analysis™ (Leadership Effectiveness Analysis is a trademark of Management Research Group).

emotional intelligence and emotional drivers. My hypothesis was that those rated more highly for authentic leadership would also score well on emotional intelligence factors, specifically, self-awareness, empathy and impulse control. In addition, I thought there would be a strong positive correlation with measures of emotional drivers such as giving (getting satisfaction from relating to others by providing them with support, affection and empathy) and expressing (satisfaction from relating to others by expressing oneself in a direct, spontaneous and emotionally uninhibited fashion).

Although my sample was small, what I found was very interesting. There was a strong relationship between the scores for authentic leadership and the two other assessment tools that I used. Specifically, I found that authentic leaders demonstrated higher empathy, showed their emotions more and had a stronger sense of well-being (happiness and contentment with their life). To a lesser but still relevant extent, they also liked to connect with groups and build positive interpersonal relationships.

To cut a long story short, authentic leadership is linked more to emotions and relationships with people than any technical skills.

You might still be wondering why authentic leadership is increasingly seen as the gold standard for leadership. I think the main reason is that the recurrent finding from many decades of research is that there is no definitive character associated with great leaders. This hasn't stopped people from trying to define good leadership in terms of competency models and blueprints. Perhaps more valuable is the research that attempts to identify what great leaders do. The best-known and most widely accepted findings are those of Jim Kouzes and Barry Posner (Kouzes and Posner, 2007), first published edition in their classic 1985 book, *The Leadership Challenge*.

Over the past thirty to forty years the two American academics have looked at hundreds of interviews, thousands of case analyses and hundreds of thousands of survey questionnaires on what leaders do when they perform at their personal best. They have identified the following five practices and ten commitments of leadership (see Figure 3.7).

I'm delighted to find that their results clearly match my humble authentic leadership model above. My 'living life with purpose and with passion' is clearly similar to their 'inspiring a shared vision'. Similarly, my 'unwavering values grounded by integrity and trust' and 'deeply connected relationships' overlap with several of the ten commitments above, while having 'high emotional intelligence' encompasses all of the five practices. And once again, Kouzes and Posner place no wait on being an 'expert' or having the best 'technical skills'.

Think of it this way. Who would you like to work for? Do you want a boss who is highly knowledgeable and an expert in their field? Or do you want someone who is going to inspire you to be your best and achieve your desired goals? Now apply your answers to yourself – and you'll conclude, as I have over the years, that to progress in most organisations, your technical skills are

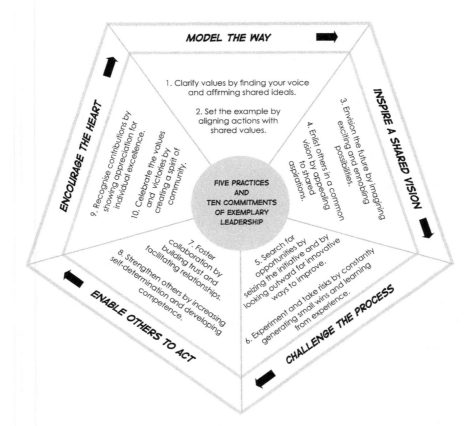

Figure 3.7 Five practices and ten commitments of exemplary leadership.
Source: Based on Kouzes & Posner (2007).

only going to get you so far. Focus instead on the authentic leadership attributes described in this chapter.

Summary of key points

- The best technical expert is not necessarily the best leader.
- Leading, motivating, inspiring and coaching others is very different to having specialist knowledge.
- Exceptional leaders are consistently described as having emotional intelligence rather than a high IQ or technical skills.
- Authentic leadership really is the gold standard for great leadership.
- Authentic leadership is highly beneficial to, for example: sales growth, employee satisfaction, high attendance at work and managerial well-being.

- Authentic leadership is about being true and genuine *and* understanding the leadership element of your responsibility to others.
- Developing yourself as an authentic leader involves:
  - Living life with purpose and passion.
  - Unwavering values grounded by integrity and trust.
  - Developing deeply connected relationships.
  - High emotional intelligence.
- Empathy results in better leadership and higher professional performance.
- Higher empathy also reduces the risk of leadership derailment.
- All this is proven by academic and practical research!

References

Avolio, B. J., Luthans, F. and Walumbwa, F. O. (2004). *Authentic Leadership: Theory Building for Veritable Sustained Performance.* Working Paper: Gallup Leadership Institute University of Nebraska–Lincoln.

Avolio, B. J., Walumbwa, F. O. and Weber, T. J. (2009). Leadership: Current Theories, Research and Future Directions. *Annual Review of Psychology,* vol. 60, pp. 421–449.

Bar-On, R. (2004). The Bar-On Emotional Quotient Inventory (EQ-I): Rationale, Description and Summary of Psychometric Properties. In G. Geher (Ed.), *Measuring Emotional Intelligence: Common Ground and Controversy.* Hauppauge, NY: Nova Science Publishers, pp. 111–142.

Clapp-Smith, R., Vogelgesang, G. R. and Avey, J. B. (2009). Authentic Leadership and Positive Psychological Capital: The Mediating Role of Trust at the Group Level of Analysis. *Journal of Leadership and Organizational Studies,* vol. 15, no. 3, pp. 227–240.

Datta, B. (2015). Assessing the Effectiveness of Authentic Leadership. *International Journal of Leadership Studies,* vol. 9. no. 1, p. 62.

Edelman (2019). *Edelman Trust Barometer Executive Summary.* Accessed: January 24, 2019. www.Edelman.com.

Frankl, V. E. (2004). *Man's Search for Meaning.* New Ed. London: Rider.

Gardner, W. L., Avolio, B. J., Luthans, F. and Walumbwa, F. O. (2005). Can You See the Real Me? A Self-based Model of Authentic Leader and Follower Development. *Leadership Quarterly,* vol. 16, pp. 343–372.

Gentry, W. A., Weber, T. J. and Sadri, G. (2007). *Empathy in the Workplace, a Tool for Effective Leadership.* Center for Creative Leadership. A white paper based on a poster that was presented at the Society of Industrial Organizational Psychology Conference, New York.

Hassan, A. and Ahmed, F. (2011). Authentic Leadership, Trust and Work Engagement. *International Journal of Human and Social Sciences,* vol. 6, no. 3, pp. 164–170.

Holt, S. and Marques, J. (2012). Empathy in Leadership: Appropriate or Misplaced? An Empirical Study on a Topic That Is Asking for Attention. *Journal of Business Ethics,* vol. 105, pp. 95–105.

Ibarra, H. (2015). The Authenticity Paradox. *Harvard Business Review,* vol. 93, pp. 52–59, January–February.

Jensen, S. M. and Luthans, F. (2006). Entrepreneurs as Authentic Leaders: Impact on Employees' Attitudes. *Leadership and Organization Development Journal,* vol. 27, no. 8, pp. 646–666.

Kouzes, J. M. and Posner, B. Z. (2007). *The Leadership Challenge*. 4th Ed. San Francisco, CA: Wiley.

Laschinger, H. K. S., Wong, C. A. and Grau, A. L. (2012). The Influence of Authentic Leadership on Newly Graduated Nurses' Experiences of Workplace Bullying, Burnout and Retention Outcomes: A Cross-sectional Study. *International Journal of Nursing Studies*, vol. 49, pp. 1266–1276.

Lipman, V. (2013). The Disturbing Link between Psychopathy and Leadership. *Forbes*, April 25.

Luthans, F. and Avolio, B. J. (2003). Authentic Leadership Development. In K. S. Cameron, J. E. Dutton and R. E. Quinn (Eds.), *Positive Organisational Scholarship*. San Francisco, CA: Berrett-Koehler, pp. 241–258.

Management Research Group. (2017). Keeping Leaders on Track. Recognising When Leaders Are at Risk for Derailment. *Webinar*. February 21, 2017. MRG. com.

Peterson, C., Park, N., Hall, N. and Seligman, M. E. P. (2009). Zest and Work. *Journal of Organisational Behaviour*, vol. 30, no. 2, pp. 161–172.

Peterson, S. J., Walumbwa, F. O., Avolio, B. J. and Hannah, S. T. (2012). The Relationship between Authentic Leadership and Follower Job Performance: The Mediating Role of Follower Positivity in Extreme Contexts. *The Leadership Quarterly*, vol. 23, pp. 502–516.

Peus, C., Wesche, J. S., Streicher, B., Braun, S. and Frey, D. (2012). Authentic Leadership: An Empirical Test of Its Antecedents, Consequences and Mediating Mechanisms. *Journal of Business Ethics*, vol. 107, pp. 331–348.

Walumbwa, F. O., Avolio, B. J., Gardner, W. L, Wernsing, T. S. and Peterson, S. J. (2008). Authentic Leadership: Development and Validation of a Theory-based Measure. *Journal of Management*, vol. 34, no. 1, pp. 89–126.

Wooley, L., Caza, A. and Levy, L. (2011). Authentic Leadership and Follower Development: Psychological Capital, Positive Work Climate and Gender. *Journal of Leadership and Organizational Studies*, vol. 18, no. 4, pp. 438–448.

Wrzesniewski, A., Berg, J. M. and Dutton, J. E. (2010). Turn the Job You Have into the Job You Want. *Harvard Business Review*, vol. 88, pp. 114–117.

4   Exposure

In Chapters 2 and 3 we saw that, despite great results, people don't always get the promotion and progression they want.

Belinda had an impressive track record for delivering results and was recruited as a Commercial Director for a household name organisation. She was excited by the role and could see great potential for improving the revenue and sales for the organisation. She worked long hours and encouraged and developed her team to focus on the income goals.

In her first year, the income and profit results had surpassed her own and the organisation's expectations. The next year she produced even better results. For Belinda, in her mind she made the connection that by working long hours she was achieving record breaking results. The organisation was very pleased with her performance as she outperformed both her colleagues and predecessor's performance. Belinda continued to spend the majority of her time on actions that increased sales for her organisation.

Belinda was ambitious and hoped and believed that this superior performance would stand her in good stead when an opportunity for promotion came. In her third year that very opportunity presented herself when the MD of the business was moving on. She along with colleagues and her predecessor threw her hat into the ring.

Belinda was unsuccessful and a colleague, Bill, who had not achieved anywhere near her results was successful. Bill had worked for the organisation for many years and was well known. He had spent many a Saturday afternoon standing around a football pitch with the other senior leaders. He had even taken up golf and regularly played golf with members of the Exec Team. Despite his inferior sales performance, Bill had great connections with the influencers for this role. Whilst Belinda was busy working all hours to get the sales in, Bill was working on his relationships with the key influencers.

Belinda was devastated. The exceptionally long hours she had worked over the past three years had meant that she had sacrificed personal relationships and had even taken its toll on her health. She believed that she would be rewarded and valued for this superior contribution. Unsurprisingly Belinda left the organisation and re-evaluated her career and approach to work.

As illustrated in the above example, professionals with lesser performance seem to get promoted – time and time again. We discovered too that, beyond a certain level in an organisation, it's building relationships and networking that helps you to secure a bigger and better job, while authentic leadership skills ensure that you excel in it. Now, I'm sorry to have to break it to you, there's something else you need to get ahead.

After decades of working with large corporations, author and consultant Harvey Coleman has concluded that there are 'unwritten rules' for getting on in an organisation (Coleman, 2005). He identifies three and the keys to advancement and promotion:

- *Perform* exceptionally well.
- Cultivate the proper *image*.
- Manage your *exposure* so the right people will know you.

Even more helpfully, Coleman claims that the three elements of his 'PIE' model don't have equal weight, and contribute to career success as follows:

- Performance – 10%.
- Image – 30%.
- Exposure – 60%.

Most of the experienced people I talk to confirm these findings. And I've seen it for myself too. Some leaders I have started to coach are highly talented individuals who work long hours and turn in a superior performance yet seem to stay stuck in their role. Equally, I know individuals who develop their image and are excellent at networking with the 'right people'. They seem to get promoted effortlessly. Undoubtedly, they have to perform as well, but not at a significantly superior level to other people (Figure 4.1).

Figure 4.1 Performance vs. building relationships.

A lot of people rail against this situation. They understand that it happens but it just doesn't seem fair to them. Indeed, human beings learn from a very early age to believe in fairness and reward based on merit. As we will see in Chapter 7, the human brain craves fairness.

However, there is a dilemma here. Whilst our brains crave fairness, at a subconscious level, we also feel more comfortable with people we believe to be 'in group'. Research has found that, when we meet people for the first time, we categorise them very quickly into friend or foe – and that we are predisposed to see more foes than friends (Rock, 2009). Transpose that to a recruitment or promotion situation, and we are more likely to feel warmer about someone we know (or at least someone we know something about) than a complete stranger. At a subconscious level, this familiar person does not trigger a fear response, which we may then rationalise with our conscious brain as 'performing better in the interview'.

Let's put that another way. The candidate believes that fairness will reign and that they will be promoted on merit, whereas the recruiter will be driven by a subconscious need to minimise threat or fear and will therefore recruit from 'in group'.

If you can understand this psychological phenomenon, it helps you to realise that getting your dream job is not about being the sycophantic networker. It is about helping the interviewer make a better decision by really knowing you. And if you were the interviewer, you would probably behave just the same way.

Working with unconscious bias

To further complicate matters, it is becoming increasingly apparent that recruitment and promotion decisions are hugely affected by unconscious bias. As the name suggests, this is about being biased against (or in favour of) certain people without really being aware of it. Unconscious bias is also beyond our control. It happens automatically and is triggered by our brain making quick judgements about people and situations based on our background, cultural environment and personal experiences. Sometimes you don't like somebody simply because they remind you of someone else! (Figure 4.2).

A recent study has identified about over 150 biases that we might use when judging others (McCormick, 2015). The following are some of the most common in the workplace:

- Affinity bias – to be biased towards people who are most like us.
- Confirmation bias – finding information that confirms our own pre-existing beliefs or assumptions.
- In-group bias – forming stereotypes and assumptions about certain groups, thus making it difficult to make objective judgement about members of those groups.

Figure 4.2 Unconscious bias.

- Halo effect (Horns effect) – to believe that everything about a person is good because you like that person. Likewise, the Horns effect is the opposite, i.e. if you don't like the person.
- Group think or conformity bias – this can be unconsciously going along with the crowd and when people are trying hard to fit into a particular group by mimicking others or holding back thoughts and opinions.
- Beauty bias – this bias is related to someone's external appearance. Typically believing that the more handsome individual will be more successful. Alternatively, if someone is more traditionally attractive, they can be hindered by their appearance, especially in the case of women. This is considered the 'bimbo effect'.

Although unconscious bias leads to 'unfair' decisions, it is natural and largely unavoidable. It affects our behaviour in subtle ways. It is not always about being negative, as we are disposed to be biased against people who are different from us and favour people who are like us. Furthermore, in situations where we are under stress, whether emotionally or cognitively, we are more like to display behaviour driven by bias. Suppressing or demonising such behaviour makes the problem worse not better, and this worsening is more likely in people who were least biased to start with.

Pendry, Driscoll and Field (2007) provided a further example by giving participants in diversity training the following father–son exercise:

A father and son were involved in a car accident in which the father was killed and the son was seriously injured. The father was pronounced dead at the scene of the accident and his body taken to a local morgue. The son was taken by ambulance to a nearby hospital and was immediately wheeled into an emergency operating room. A surgeon was called. Upon arrival, and seeing the patient the attending surgeon exclaimed, 'Oh my God, it's my son!'.

The researchers found that on their training courses over 40% of people don't get the answer. Have you? Look to the footnote to find out.[1]

Unconscious bias has been a priority for organisations, as they grapple with the issues of diversity and inclusion. Fortunately, there is action that can be taken to reduce unconscious bias, such as anonymised CVs and training. HR departments are investing significant amounts in helping employees understand their biases and how recruitment and promotion decisions are affected. Once again, we can see the vital importance of self-awareness in deeply knowing ourselves and where we might have an inherent bias.

From the candidate's point of view, it's also worth thinking through the implications of unconscious bias. There is certainly an opportunity to help recruiters become more biased in your favour by building rapport and reducing the perceived threat of not being 'in their group'.

From a recruiter's point of view, there is an even stronger case for radical self-awareness. Ask yourself whether you really understand why you favour certain candidates over others.

Unconscious bias is an issue in recruiting people and whilst this creates unfairness for certain groups, the end result can be that you have organisations where they are so homogeneous that diversity is so stifled that there is very little innovation and creativity (Figure 4.3).

I recall working with an organisation a few years ago who introduced a smart casual dress code for all employees. The chief executive started to wear a black polo top and chinos. The senior team became very obvious and visible to me as they all started to dress in exactly the same way as their Chief Exec. They just needed a logo on the shirt and it looked like a uniform!

Figure 4.3 Homogeneity of organisations.

Where is emotional intelligence in all of this?

If we accept that Coleman's PIE model is a reality in our organisations, then we can start to see how emotional intelligence can help with those two elements, image and exposure, that it's so tempting to ignore.

Let's start with image. First, there is a need to understand what constitutes a proper or appropriate image and remain authentic. You need to be able to effectively 'read' your environment to understand the desired image in order to compare your current image to it. Additionally, feedback from others is invaluable in helping you understand where you stand in comparison.

If we use our empathic influencing model (DARE) from Chapter 1, we will need to understand how at level 1 we think and perceive the world in a certain way. At level 2, we start to understand how that is different to others and how they see the world and behave accordingly. At level 3, we identify what the appropriate image is for the situation you are in. We then move up to the final level to understand the best image to have and how to show that. In terms of authenticity, clearly, we want that to be a communication challenge as opposed to a fake presentation of oneself. We want to present our true and best authentic image as a match between what we really are and what the role requires.

You can consider strategically how you are developing your image and exposure with key stakeholders from a managing your career perspective in the particular organisation you are working for. At a more tactical level, it will help if every time you go to a meeting to remind yourself about what do you want them to say about you when you leave that meeting. Using the DARE empathic influencing will assist you in achieving that.

If you consider the exposure part of the formula, it follows that once you are clear on the (authentic) image you want to portray, your objective will then be how you let others know you and how you are going to influence them using DARE.

Summary of key points

- Performance, image and exposure (PIE) all contribute to advancement and promotion.
- Performance is only a small contributing factor, while exposure is the biggest and image is in between.
- There is a paradox in that we want and expect fairness and to be rewarded on merit, yet we choose other people by minimising the threat and fear in the brain and selecting 'in group'.
- Unconscious bias plays a major part in recruitment and promotion.
- You can use empathic influencing to help your interviewers overcome unconscious bias and reduce their brains' threat responses.
- Empathic influencing helps with developing image and exposure.

Note

1   The surgeon was the boy's mother.

References

Coleman, H. (2005). *Empowering Yourself.* 2nd ed. Dubuque, IA: Kendall/Hunt Publishing Company.

McCormick, H. (2015). *The Real Effects of Unconscious Bias in the Workplace.* Chapel Hill, NC: Kenen-Flagler Business School, Executive Development, University of North Carolina.

Pendry, L., Driscoll, D. M. and Field, S. C. (2007). Diversity Training: Putting Theory into Practice. *Journal of Occupational and Organisational Psychology*, vol. 80, no. 1, pp. 25–50.

Rock, D. (2009). *Your Brain at Work.* New York: HarperCollins, pp. 161–169.

Part II
Authenticity

5   How to develop empathic influencing and still be authentic

In Chapter 3 we talked about authentic leadership as the gold standard for leadership. And now more than ever, it's the best and most successful way of being a leader. As more corporate scandals and questions over business morality emerge, the greater the demand for a different type of leadership.

Being the best version of you

The question you are probably asking at this point is: surely if I want to be an authentic leader and I just don't have empathic influencing skills, then wouldn't it be *inauthentic* to try and develop them? However, as we highlighted in Chapter 3, being an authentic leader is not the same as being your authentic self. When you are leading others – and indeed in any relationship – you always need to develop yourself. It's not about a wholesale change of who you are; it's about being the best possible version of yourself.

What does that mean in practice? First and foremost, you need to have excellent self-awareness so that you know what your strengths are. You need to make sure that you are in a role that plays mainly to those strengths. You also need to be aware of what you love doing. Whilst this is probably also something you are good at, it is worth reflecting on what has given you genuine joy recently. Was it solving that particular problem, analysing those particular details or achieving that long-targeted goal?

However, self-awareness also comes with an understanding of where you need to develop. This means looking at feedback from performance reviews, colleagues and friends, as well as considering what you 'know' about yourself. By using both of these strategies to work out who you really are, you can figure out where you could be even better and achieve your own personal best. It is not about changing fundamental aspects of your personality (Figures 5.1 and 5.2).

To illustrate this point, I was once asked to coach a board member of a large, well-known IT company. I was given the information that, whilst he was technically very good, he needed to be more forthcoming at board meetings and also to engage more with his team. We started with an initial coaching session and he also completed

Figure 5.1 Self-awareness – understanding where you need to develop.

some psychometric tests, including a personality profile and an emotional intelligence assessment.

We talked about what he did really well and what he thought he needed to work on. He described being uncomfortable speaking out in the boardroom and also approaching and connecting with his people. When I probed a little further, it turned out that the reason for both of these limiting behaviours was a belief that he did not have anything interesting to offer.

From his psychometrics, it was clear he was not an extrovert and the profile suggested he would be described as a shy person. Our goal in coaching was therefore not to transform him into an extrovert. That just wouldn't work. Can you imagine this person suddenly becoming the life and soul of the party? Even if he succeeded, he would look inauthentic and damage the trust of his colleagues.

The emotional intelligence assessment also revealed that he was very low in self-regard and this was supported by the comments he had made in our first session. Whilst I knew that he was unlikely to become an extrovert through coaching, I was certain that he was capable of valuing himself and feeling worthy enough to make that contribution to the board and to feel comfortable approaching his people. This is what he worked on – and with great success. Yes, he found out that people did want to hear from him and were interested in him. His old beliefs were unfounded.

Figure 5.2 Becoming the extrovert.

Being the best version of you is about working on your areas for development whilst not changing the core of who you are – and so remaining authentic. This may not be how you approach things currently, but it's a matter of becoming more effective in a very specific way without changing who you are as a person.

It is about having that deep self-awareness and knowing which attributes help you to be truly effective and also which behaviours are both damaging to others and derailing for yourself (Figure 5.3).

When you think about it, you weren't born an accountant, lawyer, IT professional or any other type of technical specialist. These were just skills that you learnt along the way. Empathic influencing is just another skill to be

Figure 5.3 Self-awareness of damaging behaviours.

developed and, coupled with your technical skills, it will unlock significant benefits at higher levels in your organisation – and your life.

Empathy and emotion in authenticity

As we saw in Chapter 3, empathy and emotion play an essential role in authentic leadership. Furthermore, the five practices and ten commitments defined by Kouzes and Posner in Chapter 3 cannot be achieved, unless you engage emotionally with your colleagues (Kouzes and Posner, 2007) (Figure 5.4).

From my own experience of coaching I see this as the key differentiator between good and great leaders – and those leading happy and successful lives.

Jonathan was the COO of a large manufacturing organisation. He led a number of teams and in terms of operations performance he truly excelled. Manufacturing costs were down, efficiency and productivity were high, and his colleagues and chief exec saw him as someone who always delivered what he promised. Jonathan was considered to be a good leader of his people.

Another organisation had relocated its operations to near where this company was based. They wanted to attract local people and were offering the same pay rates but slightly better benefits, such as private healthcare and a better pension. They also were known for their company value of caring for their employees.

Jonathan's organisation was concerned about losing staff to this other company. Their location meant that attracting quality people was a constant battle and they wanted to retain their workforce. A few people had already gone to the other organisation, which unsettled others. Furthermore, the 'leavers' kept in touch with their old colleagues and were talking about how they felt valued and appreciated in their new jobs.

The chief executive could not understand why there was a particular outflow of talent from Jonathan's teams. They had excellent performance and he thought that they must

Figure 5.4 Engage emotionally with your colleagues.

feel proud to work for such a successful operation. In his attempt to understand, he commissioned an employee opinion survey. The results were disappointing. Although Jonathan's area had the best performance in terms of the organisation's key performance indicators on measures of productivity, costs etc. his was the worst performing area on the employee opinion survey in terms of morale. Indeed, the results suggested that Jonathan's people felt undervalued and unappreciated. Although the camaraderie between colleagues was positive, there was a lot of criticism of their leaders.

Only the week before, the CEO had just attended a conference on the importance of well-being in the workforce and the pivotal role that leaders play. Some research had been presented demonstrating that people join great organisations but leave because of poor managers. It was clear that he had to deal with the situation head on if the impressive results were to be sustained. He decided that he and his leadership team would undertake coaching, including a 360-degree assessment by their teams.

Jonathan met with his coach and in his first session just couldn't understand what was required of him. He delivered results and the organisation was doing well, so he considered himself a good leader. But, as the findings from the 360 came back, he was in for a shock. His people complained that they never got any thanks and when they went the extra mile by, for example, working late, it was never acknowledged. They felt like a number rather than a human being – and, heaven forbid, if they had a personal issue stopping them for performing at 100%! There was no discussion about their career aspirations, let alone their life goals. Their jobs offered no meaning or satisfaction. They simply did what was required and would only do more when pressured to. All in all, they felt demotivated and stressed.

Reading the comments Jonathan felt surprised on a couple of counts: first that people felt so strongly and second that these things were so important to them. He didn't get any positive feedback from the chief executive either, but then he didn't feel he needed it. He measured his success by his own high standards and didn't need others to recognise them. It was a complete eye opener to realise how his team felt and what they wanted from him.

Over the following six to twelve months, Jonathan worked with his coach to develop his emotional intelligence. He started by really trying to understand people, particularly those who were most different from him. He used that understanding to develop a new individualised leadership approach. He then learnt to communicate in a way that engaged people. This required him to use more emotional expression, which in turn meant he had to understand not just what he thought but also how he felt. During this time, others started to perceive him as 'warmer', as he showed a genuine interest in them. He developed his own understanding of his own sense of purpose in life and passionately told people about his newfound 'why'. He expressed his values and gave examples of how he had made decisions based on those. He encouraged his people to think about their own purpose in life and how their jobs helped them achieve it.

The employee opinion survey was repeated the following year and the operations area reported a huge increase. Jonathan had gone from being a good leader to a great one. Furthermore, the outflow of talent was stemmed. In fact, people were requesting transfers to Jonathan's teams.

Jonathan's discovery that he needed something more to be an authentic leader matches the findings from the research I did with my clients to investigate the relationship between authentic leadership and emotional intelligence and drivers.

My research confirmed that authentic leaders have high levels of empathy and well-being (happiness and contentment with their life), desire to have a close connection with others and believe in the importance of showing their emotions. To a lesser but still significant extent, they are likely to get satisfaction from working in groups and develop good interpersonal relationships.

If we buy into the idea of authentic leadership, it follows that we need to demonstrate empathic influencing and emotional engagement to be successful. I'd even go so far as to say that authentic leadership with the above two facets is the only way to move from good to great.

Learn to make authentic choices

Choice is something that we all aspire to, whether over what we purchase, how we live our lives or how we behave. Choice gives us autonomy, which has been shown to be important for our psychological well-being. In studies where people could choose how much pain relief to administer, researchers found that those who had the choice needed significantly less medication than those who had no choice (4.94 mg/kg as opposed to 12.17 mg/kg) (Mackie et al., 1991). See also Krummenacher et al. (2009) showing how expectations and beliefs can modulate the experience of pain (Krummenacher et al., 2009). Similarly, a 2009 article by Stern, Dhanda and Hazuda in the *Journal of Psychosomatic Research* found that one of the biggest causes of stress is perceived helplessness. It seems that feeling in control is fundamental to how our brain interprets our experiences. Even a slight sense of autonomy can significantly change how we perceive an event (Stern et al., 2009).

When you stop to think about it, there are very few things that you don't have choice over. So often you might say that you *have to* do things like working late or doing a particular job. The reality is that you don't have to. You just don't choose the consequences of not doing it. Sometimes, it's worth considering what your genuine alternatives are – and you'll see that you've rejected a less favourable outcome. Although your course of action may remain the same, you'll realise that you are in position of choice – an autonomous position.

Once you recognise this, it will help you to think and feel that you have control over your life. Of course, you might not want to work late and miss your daughter's concert, but the cost of not working late might be that you let someone else down on something essential you have committed to. By not delivering on this occasion, you might mean have to work even harder to build their trust in future – and spend even less time with your family. But there might be a third option. Your daughter needs you at the concert. It's something she'll remember when you are old and grey. If you explain to your colleagues that – just this once – you will be a day late because your daughter needs you, they may understand. They will consider the incident in the context of the past, present and future. And, crucially, you will be fully aware of the conscious choice you are making.

The issue of choice becomes even more interesting when we start to look at how we behave. People frequently believe that, because they have done something for years, maybe even decades, it will be nigh on impossible to change.

One thing I ask my clients to consider is whether they believe they have control over their minds. If the answer is 'yes', then they can also choose to behave in a certain way – a fact that's borne out by neuroscience, as we'll see in the next part, Chapters 6 and 7. In our everyday lives that might be choosing not to react to someone or something that has been said. It might be choosing not to get upset or it might be choosing to show any emotion at all. The key is to have excellent self-awareness. If you understand what you are thinking and feeling, you can deal with it accordingly.

By first of all understanding what you are thinking and feeling, you can then determine what your range of responses might be. Then you can decide what the most appropriate reaction would be for the outcome you are wanting. I encourage clients to think about the choice between going through a red (angry) door or a green (constructive) door. Which door is going to take them to where they want to go and the outcome they want to achieve (Figure 5.5)?

Figure 5.5 Choosing the red or green door.

This is particularly challenging for people who struggle with impulse control. They will always have reacted in a default way and, more often than not, regretted their reaction. It has been found that the ability to self-manage and self-regulate leads to success in life– and is absolutely essential for leaders. It is particularly important at times when leaders are expected to provide consistency (a measure of certainty for the brain). Generally, it is agreed upon that people do not work well for leaders who are volatile and unpredictable. Choosing the most appropriate response for the situation is crucial for both leader and follower – or indeed in any type of human relationship.

The most extreme examples of self-regulation occur during torture. From Victor Frankl's account of Holocaust survivors (in *Man's Search for Meaning*) to the books written by former SAS sergeant Andy McNab where there are many examples of the mind controlling extreme pain inflicted on the body. In addition, Victor Frankl describes how those who had a clear reason to live were more likely to survive the concentration camps. His view was: 'When you have a "why", you can endure any "how"' (Frankl, 2004).

If reactions can be controlled in such extreme circumstances, then surely, it's possible in everyday life.

I had to employ such skills a few years ago, when I was harassed and stalked. For a few months I was fearful for myself and for my family and friends, as my harasser set about trying (in his words) 'to destroy my life and everything I stood for'. I was very fearful about leaving my home and hyper-vigilant about danger. I was experiencing chest pains, loss of sleep and appetite, and suffering from eczema for the first time in my life. I realised that the stress and anxiety would kill me (if he didn't first). So, I made a conscious choice to take control of my mind. As soon as I woke up every morning, I became acutely aware of the negative thoughts and shut them down. I reframed what was happening to me as best I could. I derived strength from believing that, whilst this person could take everything from me, my values were strong and I would not be broken. I controlled my mind to choose a different way of being under extreme circumstances. It was stressful and hard work but I continued to function without breaking. Although I never want to experience this extreme stress again, I did learn the power of being able to control my emotions and to a certain extent my outcomes by controlling my mind and making choices that would support me. It enabled me to be resilient at the time, build my resilience overall and recover from a negative life event.

We all need to be true and authentic to ourselves if we are going to become the best we can possibly be.

Clearly too, choice and self-regulation play an important part in empathic influencing. If we want to get the best out of others, we don't just react to what they say or do. Instead, we take a conscious choice to say something that will land well with them.

We have a choice. All we have to do is recognise it – and make the best authentic decision. We will probably start with an initial evaluation of our choices: a combination of rational analysis and 'feel'. Having identified the right choice, the next step using the DARE model of empathic influencing is to think through how that decision will impact others. If you were standing in their shoes would you see it positively or negatively? Next, how is their worldview different from yours? So how would they see it? You can only answer that final question if you have a great empathic relationship with them.

Summary of key points

- Develop deep self-awareness to be the best version of yourself.
- Empathic influencing is just another skill to learn; it is not an inherent trait.
- Truly authentic leaders have higher empathy and well-being and connect well with their people.
- Choice gives us autonomy which creates a positive 'toward' state in our brain.
- We have choice over most things if we think about it and the conscious choices we are making.
- We also have choice over how we behave, albeit with effective impulse control.
- To develop our empathic influencing skills we do need to understand how to employ choice over our actions and decisions.

References

Frankl, V. E. (2004). *Man's Search for Meaning*. New Ed. London: Rider.

Kouzes, J. M. and Posner, B. Z. (2007). *The Leadership Challenge*. 4th Ed. San Francisco, CA: Wiley.

Krummenacher, P., Candia, V., Folkers, G., Schedlowski, M. and Schonbackler, G. (2009). Prefrontel Cortex Modulates Placebo Analgesia. *Pain*, vol. 148, no. 3, pp. 368–374.

Mackie, A. M., Coda, B. C. and Hill, H. F. (1991). Adolescents Use Patient-controlled Analgesia Effectively for Relief from Prolonged Oropharyngeal Mucositis Pain. *Pain*, vol. 46, no. 3, pp. 265–269.

Stern, S. L., Dhanda, R. and Hazuda, H. P. (2009). Helplessness Predicts the Development of Hypertension in Older Mexican and European Americans. *Journal of Psychosomatic Research*, vol. 67, pp. 333–337.

6 The dark side of empathic influencing

In Chapter 5 I talked about the benefits of empathic influencing at work and at home. Empathic influencing can help you to achieve many good things for the people around you and for yourself. They will feel motivated, understood and valued. You will be connecting at a deeper level and performing at a higher level. Your leadership may even have moved from good to great. By understanding what is behind people's behaviour, you will respond to the root cause rather than what appears on the surface. To illustrate this, I will share a personal experience from early in my career.

When I was in my late twenties, I joined my father's consulting business. Prior to that, I had been a high-flyer at Ford Motor Company where I had progressed rapidly. I had then done an MBA and worked at a large consultancy. My father's business employed a number of people, including Will, the operations director. Initially I worked for him delivering consultancy projects. After a few months I found out that Will was going to see my father and negatively reporting about me and my work. I didn't understand it, as I had great feedback from my clients. Although I was doing work I didn't particularly enjoy, I didn't think it was fair to be negative about me. My initial reaction was that I needed to show Will just how great I was and what worthwhile experience I was bringing. I prepared to impress him with my credentials during our next meeting.

A few days later I happened to be chatting to our office manager. We were talking about how future work would be resourced and she casually mentioned that Will had said, 'Well, it won't be long until there are more bright young people in like Ruth.' I was suddenly enlightened.

Will felt threatened. I was young and intelligent and that was the future. It was a direction that might not include him. His comments to my father were borne out of fear and vulnerability about his value and ultimately his job security. If I had embarked on the conversation I had planned, bigging up myself and my experience, it would have just made things worse. I needed to respond to the root issue here — his vulnerability. I made a 180-degree change of approach. When I met Will, we talked about his own vast experience. I made him feel good and positive about what he brought. Even though I was the follower, not the leader, I helped him to feel secure. The negative comments about me went away and we developed a strong working relationship.

I encourage my clients to reflect on the people they have a relationship with. I ask them to think deeply about why those people might be behaving in a certain way – and perhaps even to look at other examples of their behaviour in different settings. By finding the Achilles heel, my clients can protect it and ensure positive communication and a good relationship, rather than attacking it and exacerbating the situation (Figure 6.1).

However, the fundamental assumption is that my clients' motives and intentions are positive, and that they genuinely feel some empathy. And, as we will see in Chapter 9, it is also having more than just cognitive empathy. But there is also a dark side to empathy, which has negative outcomes. Let's say someone is excellent at reading other people. As well as knowing how to influence them, he or she knows exactly what will hurt them. These skills are then used to manipulate others. Such a person is effectively demonstrating psychopathic behaviour – and with aplomb. As we saw in Chapter 3, there may already be a disproportionate number of psychopaths in the leadership population (Lipman, 2013). Developing empathic influencing skills is not a means of adding to that number!

The key here is to have the good values and strong ethics needed to become the kind of authentic leader we discovered in Chapter 3. Even without any leadership

Figure 6.1 Making ethical choices with others' Achilles heel.

responsibility, it is better to use our values for the greater good, rather than acting in a manipulative and Machiavellian manner to achieve only selfish ends.

In practice, this means understanding your true purpose and intention. When you become very good at reading and influencing people, you need to be clear about why you are doing so. Is it to have a great conversation and connection with this person? Or is it to achieve something for yourself? Remember that at some point in the future the other person may feel manipulated. This could hugely impact your trustworthiness. Honesty with yourself is crucial.

From my many, many experiences of coaching leaders, I have felt that the outcomes of our discussions were for positive intent in all but a handful of cases. In these instances, we identified how the person my client wanted to influence might be feeling, what their Achilles heel might be and how to work with that. My gut feel was that the intention was malicious. Likewise, as a young coach with the ear of a powerful chief executive, I think that I too was manipulated once or twice. Both types of experience left a bad taste, although I learnt a lot from them. I am now alert to the 'dark side' of empathic influencing and avoid those who show signs of it.

It is interesting to look at what distinguishes some of the greatest leaders of the twentieth century. Holt and Marques (2012) refer to what the researcher Schilling did in 2010 as part of a Ph.D. dissertation. This research looked at leaders such as John F. Kennedy, Martin Luther King, Jr., Mahatma Gandhi, Mikhail Gorbachev, Nelson Mandela and Lech Walesa. Whilst they were often labelled as charismatic, their levels of empathy, emotional intelligence, commitment, inspirational motivation and trustworthiness were outstanding and helped to make them the remarkable individuals they became (Schilling, 2010).

Summary of key points

- Success comes from deeply understanding the other people you work with, including their fears and what makes them react the way they do.
- Deep understanding of others needs to be employed in a positive and ethical way.
- Be clear about your own intentions. Be scrupulously honest and deeply self-aware.
- High empathy is found in remarkable leaders.

References

Holt, S. and Marques, J. (2012). Empathy in Leadership: Appropriate or Misplaced? An Empirical Study on a Topic That Is Asking for Attention. *Journal of Business Ethics*, vol. 105, pp. 95–105.

Lipman, V. (2013). The Disturbing Link between Psychopathy and Leadership. *Forbes*, April 25.

Schilling, L. (2010). *A Historical Analysis of the Relationship between Charisma and the Making of Great Leaders*. Ph.D. Dissertation, Walden University, Minneapolis, MN.

Part III
The science bit

7   Humans are not rational

There seems to be a huge misconception amongst highly technical people that humans are rational and will behave in a logical and consistent way. In fact, most of us are surprised when people don't take the most logical course of action – and this is particularly true if we consider ourselves to be highly logical.

Furthermore, people often claim to be quite uncomfortable when someone appears illogical, irrational or, worse, emotional – all of which can lead to inconsistent behaviour. That discomfort is easily understood once we know how the brain works. When people don't behave as we expect or predict, it triggers a threat response. The human brain loves certainty and predictability.

The following text comes from a famous study. Can you read it?

I cnduo't bvleiee taht I culod aulaclty uesdtannrd waht I was rdnaieg. Unisg the icndeblire pweor of the hmuan mnid, aocdcrnig to rseecrah at Cmabrigde Uinervtisy, it dseno't mttaer in waht oderr the lterets in a wrod are, the olny irpoamtnt tihng is taht the frsit and lsat ltteer be in the rhgit pclae.

(Interestingly, it appears this did not originate at Cambridge University and has been tracked back to a Dr Rawlinson who was undertaking his Ph.D. at Nottingham University on 'The significance of letter position in word recognition' (1976)).

The brain is masterful at putting patterns together into a cohesive whole to tell a good story. The above is a good example but consider how many times in your day-to-day life you don't know all the facts and just fill in the blanks to make sense of the situation. The conclusion of neuroscientists is that prediction may be a primary function of the brain – and you will put yourself in a position where things appear to make sense to achieve that certainty. Conversely, when that doesn't happen, the uncertainty will cause you some anxiety.

Interplay of our rational and emotional brain

When looking at how the human brain responds, researchers have found that ambiguity is off-putting and certainty is rewarding (Whalen, 1998; Sarinopulos et al., 2010). Indeed, it is enough to receive information that only leads to more certainty. This is because certainty is less-resource intensive for the brain, which does not need to engage its energy-hungry prefrontal cortex. Furthermore, uncertainty arouses the brain's limbic system, which means further additional effort. Studies have found that only when there is damage to one region of the prefrontal cortex do people behave totally rationally and have no bias for certainty (Hsu et al., 2005). So, whilst brains crave certainty and like *other* people to behave predictably, our *own* brains don't always help us to behave rationally. It's a classic double whammy. Of course, brains are incredibly complex organs. I like to simplify this amazing structure as the emotional brain (the older limbic system) and the rational brain (the newer prefrontal cortex). It is endlessly fascinating to observe in people – and indeed ourselves – the interplay between these two parts of our brains. It is clearly erroneous to believe that the rational brain is totally in charge of us and our behaviour (Figure 7.1).

Figure 7.1 Rational and emotional brain.

When we consider our amygdala (which is in our limbic brain), we find further illustration of why humans are not rational. The word 'amygdala' comes from the Greek word for almond and this part of the brain is an almond-shaped structure. Think of it as our own personal alarm system. It scans the environment and is sensitive to potential threats. Within milliseconds, it can elicit a fight, flight or freeze response before you are even consciously aware of reacting. Furthermore, it can override the thinking part of our brain – our prefrontal cortex. People who suffer from anxiety, be it specific or generalised, benefit from knowing whether their amygdala or pre-frontal cortex is initiating the response. The strategies for dealing with each are very different. When their amygdala is involved, it is very clear that a rational, logic-based approach will just not work. They cannot simply think themselves out of feeling anxious.

The good news is that, unlike other animals, most of us do have an effec-tive prefrontal cortex. In most human brains, the prefrontal cortex is 29% of our cortex whereas in most animals it is minuscule. For example, in a chim-panzee it is just 17% of their cortex, a dog is 7% and a cat is 3%.

If my dog sees something that startles him, e.g. a paper bag that just seems to jump out of the bushes, he won't engage his rational brain and think: 'What's the likelihood of that being dangerous – it's only a paper bag?' His limbic system will go on alert and he will feel fear. Conversely, when humans are functioning well and experience a similar surprise, they engage their prefrontal cortex. They will make a logical decision and behave rationally (Figure 7.2).

However, the nature of the brain is such that the limbic system is older and, crucially, faster than the prefrontal cortex. We may feel something

Figure 7.2 Dog and monster.

before we can think our way out of it. Depending on where we are in our life or day, that feeling may end up hijacking our amygdala, making rational thought harder to achieve. To make matters worse, our prefrontal cortex is the 'Goldilocks' area of our brain (Arnsten, 1998). It likes the environment to be 'just right' to operate effectively. Too little stress and it's not effective; too much stress and it switches off completely. We can see this happening for ourselves in organisations where there are high levels of stress. People react emotionally to each other and misinterpret others' words and actions. We can start to see why humans are less rational than we would like.

Now consider how this plays out in terms of how we act and make decisions. Let's say we have a major decision to make, such as choosing which new house to buy or identifying whether someone we just went out with might be Mr or Ms Right!

Maybe we write down all the criteria that are important. We might even weight them, assess the options against them and come up with a score. We look at the resulting logical option and then think: 'No that doesn't feel right!' How often do people say the person they are happily married to is not who they would have described as their ideal partner before meeting them? How often do people buy a house that just 'feels right'?

Many years ago, I was working for a large organisation, which developed an assessment centre to recruit graduates. The assessment process included a number of individual and group tasks for the candidates, as well as a number of interviews. Each activity was scored against a series of competencies. At the end of the two days, a panel including HR staff and senior managers sat down to decide who should be made an offer and who to reject. It was interesting that some of the highest scoring candidates were rejected, as the senior managers stated that they would not want that person working for them. Whilst this raises questions about inherent and unconscious bias, it also illustrates how illogical human decision-making can be.

Another fascinating lesson from research is about free will. We assume we have free will, but knowledge of the brain suggests that this is not the case. In 1983, psychologist Benjamin Libet conducted an experiment that looked at how long it took people to engage in a voluntary activity (in the experiment it was to raise a finger) (Libet et al., 1983). The researchers found that the brain sent a signal 0.3 seconds before the subjects were even aware that it had. At this point, they could indeed choose to raise a finger but only had 0.2 seconds to make the choice. What is interesting is that our brain is busy sending signals out without us knowing. We do have the choice, but only to act on the impulses or not. It is more a case of 'free won't' (coined by Jeffrey Schwartz) rather than 'free will' (Schwartz, 2003) (Figure 7.3).

We can now see why animals act more on their impulses than we humans. We can also see that when we are tired or stressed, we may have less capacity to control our impulses and urges. Most importantly, we can understand why we don't behave rationally in a range of situations.

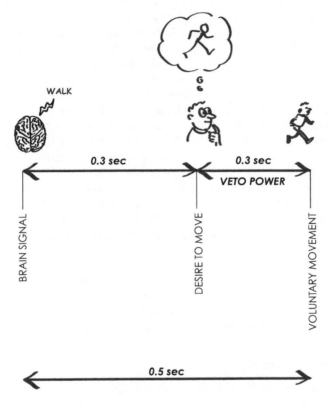

Figure 7.3 Free won't.

Living in a completely rational world

The workings of the brain stop us from being highly rational, but would we really welcome the prospect of being completely rational? Let's imagine that we're all robots, behaving predictably and logically, a bit like Spock in *Star Trek*. On the one hand, we can predict other people's behaviour, which will give our brains some certainty. There will be clarity and transparency in all decisions. There will be less stress from relationships. We can spend time on the things that yield value to us. On the other hand, when we see an old lady fall in the street, we won't go to help her. We will just get on with our day, as there is no personal benefit to helping her. What's more, there is no place for emotion, novelty and excitement.

Whilst the brain craves certainty, it also likes the release of dopamine from a certain amount of novelty. We all know that we quite like new experiences sometimes and not the same old all the time. We also like to connect with others. And when that works well, our brain releases oxytocin, which is another feel-good chemical.

There are numerous examples of people behaving illogically and yet creating the kind of society we want to live in. Take the Brownlee brothers, both former world-champion triathletes. In September 2016 they were competing in the World Triathlon Series in Cozumel, Mexico. Jonny Brownlee was ahead and on course to win, but within a few hundred metres of the finish line his legs started to wobble. At this point Alistair Brownlee came around the corner, with another competitor hot on his heels, and saw his brother collapsing. If behaving logically, Alistair would have run past his collapsing brother and won the race. He didn't. Instead, he put his brother's arm over his shoulder and ran across the finish line with him allowing the other competitor to win. As Alastair stated to the *Guardian Sport* (2016):

> *If it happened to anyone I would have helped them across the line, because it's an awful position to be in. If he'd conked out before the finish line and there wasn't medical support, it could have been really dangerous. It was a natural human reaction to my brother but for anyone I would have done the same thing. I think it's as close to death as you can be in sport.*

Whilst this story illustrates the illogicality of human behaviour, it also provoked an outpouring of support and admiration from the public throughout the world. It restored a sense of faith in human behaviour and proved that people can follow a positive code that is not always rational.

In pursuit of fairness

Research into the brain's response to fairness demonstrates that we do not behave rationally in this respect either. In 2008, Golnaz Tabibnia and her team showed that people would prefer to receive no money than to accept an 'unfair' offer of money. The rational response would be to take something, as that is more valuable than nothing. But the desire for fairness was played out in the experiment, just as it is every day in the world around us. Just think of the people who engage in lengthy legal disputes based on 'principle' (Tabibnia et al., 2008).

And what about intuition in a rational world?

Another downside of the highly logical and analytical approach is that it downplays the role of intuition in our lives. Intuition can be defined as 'a thing that one knows or considers likely from instinctive feeling rather than conscious reasoning'. It is accessing our unconscious thinking rather than the conscious logical and rational processing.

As we've already seen, we need intuition to buy a house or to find Mr/Ms Right. And there are many other situations where we rely on our 'gut feeling' to guide our decisions or actions. By clinging strongly to analysis and logic, we ignore and sometimes even fight vital signs in our body that are suggesting a different direction (Figure 7.4).

Figure 7.4 Gut feeling.

Research has even found that for some decisions our unconscious is far better at making decisions that our conscious rational brain. Dijksterhuis and Nordgren found that our unconscious thinking is a far better approach for complex decisions than conscious thinking. The latter been preferable for more simple decisions. Furthermore, they point out that it is important to understand how the intuitive thought arose. Was it truly a snap judgement with no processing at a deeper level or based on the result of considerable unconscious thought having had access to relevant information that suddenly presents itself? (Dijksterhuis and Nordgren, 2006).

In Malcom Gladwell's book *Blink* (Gladwell, 2006), he describes how a lieutenant fire fighter intuitively knew to get his fire fighters out of a burning building. Within seconds of them exiting the building, the floor they had been standing on collapsed, which would have resulted in multiple deaths and injuries of his team. At the time and for many years after, the lieutenant credited extrasensory perception (ESP) for this and other life-saving snap decisions. However, when asked to go over in minute detail the occurrences of that particular incident, it became clear that his unconscious mind was rapidly processing information than his conscious mind was unable to with the same speed. For example, the fire was not responding as a kitchen fire was supposed to. The fire didn't respond to water, it was a lot hotter than he would have expected and it was quiet, which didn't correspond to the amount of heat in the room. It transpired that the fire was actually in the basement. His unconscious mind had calculated that before he could consciously make the connections (Gladwell, 2006).

From personal experience I have ignored my intuition at great cost. Once I met someone who aroused a strong sense of mistrust from the moment I shook her hand. When I look back, in addition to this general gut-feeling there were individual pieces of contradictory information that were there and I chose to ignore them. Instead, I listened to rational presentations appealing to my analytical brain. I even berated myself for believing that my reticence was down to being risk averse. I ended up investing hundreds of thousands of pounds in one of her projects. Of course, my intuition knew something that my analytical brain didn't. Years later I, along with many others, lost thousands of pounds (approximately £4.5 million between us), and eventually she went to prison for fraud. As we saw earlier, sometimes our emotional brains know things that are not yet apparent to our logical brains!

Intuition is not some magical process. As Dijksterhuis, Nordgren and Gladwell suggest it occurs when our unconscious mind rapidly assimilates information and experience, making connections and informing us – often via our body – about what we need to do.

I am reminded of one of my clients, who was caught up in the Hillsborough disaster. In a split second she felt that she had to turn left. Had she turned right, she would not have been able to tell me the story. Perhaps, similar to the firefighter in the above example, it was her intuition rapidly assessing the situation and urging her to go one way – and importantly she responded to it.

Sometimes if we think or analyse too much, we don't make our best decision. There are numerous stories like this one, where people seem to just know things. They sense it. To think about the irrational in a rational way, perhaps they are concertinaing their experience into a second – faster than they can logically process it – to get an intuitive answer.

For people who are analytical, it is a constant battle to switch off the rational part of the brain and truly listen to their intuition. If you are one of them, it's a skill that's certainly worth developing in order to make better decisions. It may sound a bit 'woo woo' to start with. However, by engaging with your self-awareness and the reactions of your body – perhaps tenseness in your shoulders or tightness in your stomach – you will be using more of the information available to you, which should help you make better decisions.

This was described perfectly by a senior director I was coaching. He told me that he was highly rational and logical, and yet, as he got older he increasingly listened to what his body was telling him. He found that he gets a feeling in his stomach telling him something isn't right. He said that he doesn't know what it is and can't analyse it – just that he needs to listen and respond to it. He also found that, without ruminating on it, the reason tended to emerge. Listening to this intuition had stood him in great stead many a time.

I believe that good decision-making isn't just about operating one way or the other. I think it is about using an effective interplay of the two systems that operate in our brains: The X system and the C system. They correspond with our older limbic brain (Reflexive or X) and our newer prefrontal cortex (Reflective or C). The X system is automatic, spontaneous and more sensory, with fast parallel processing. The C system is controlled, intentional and slower, with serial processing. As I mentioned earlier, the prefrontal cortex is resource-intensive, that is, it uses a lot of energy, which is a clear drawback.

If you consider yourself more logical than emotional, it's time to counter-balance your natural tendency by listening more to your intuition. Likewise, if you are a highly intuitive type, I encourage you to engage your analytical brain and employ more logical approaches to decision-making. Either way, you have an important advantage if you can listen effectively to both your X and C systems.

Summary of key points

- Humans are not rational and do not always behave logically.
- Our brains love predictability and crave certainty, as well as looking for patterns.
- Whilst we like predictability in others, our older limbic brain doesn't help us to behave in a predictable way.
- We often make decisions and choices based on what feels right, rather than the logical analysis of several options.
- High levels of stress or tiredness also inhibit the effective working of our rational and logical brain.
- A fully rational world may not be the world we want to live in.
- Our response to fairness also shows that we do not always behave rationally.
- Our intuition sometimes 'knows' something before we have rationally processed it.
- Listening to our intuition can be very helpful.
- The interplay of both our rational and emotional brains makes us highly effective.

References

Arnsten, A. F. T. (1998). The Biology of Being Frazzled. *Science*, vol. 280, pp. 1711–1712.

Dijksterhuis, A. and Nordgren, L. F. (2006). A Theory of Unconscious Thought. *Perspectives of Psychological Science*, vol. 1, no. 2, pp. 95–109.

Gladwell, M. (2006). *Blink: The Power of Thinking Without Thinking*. London: Penguin Books.

Hsu, M., Bhatt, M., Adophs, R., Tranel, D. and Camerer, C. F. (2005). Neural Systems Responding to Degrees of Uncertainty in Human Decision Making. *Science*, vol. 310, pp. 1680–1683.

Libet, B., Gleason, C. A., Wright E. W. and Pearl, D. K. (1983, September). Time of Conscious Intention to Act in Relation to Onset of Cerebral Activity (Readiness-potential). The Unconscious Initiation of a Freely Voluntary Act. *Brain*, vol. 106, pp. 623–642.

Rawlinson, G. (1976). *The Significance of Letter Position in Word Recognition*. PH.D, University of Nottingham, Nottingham.

Sarinopoulos, I., Grupe, D. W., Mackiewicz, K. L., Herrington J. D., Lor, M., Steege, E. E. and Nitschke, J. B. (2010, April 1). Uncertainty during Anticipation Modulates Neural Responses to Aversion in Human Insula and Amygdala. *Cerebral Cortex*, vol. 20, no. 4, pp. 929–940.

Schwartz, J. (2003). *The Mind and the Brain*. New York: Harper Perennial.

Tabibnia, G., Satpute, A. B. and Lieberman, M. D. The Sunny Side of Fairness Activates Reward Circuitry (and Disregarding Unfairness Activates Self-control and Circuitry). *Psychological Science*, vol. 19, pp. 339–347.

The Guardian Sport. (2016, September 19). Alistair Brownlee Gives Up Chance to Win Triathlon and Helps Brother Over Line. *The Guardian*. Accessed: December 13, 2018. https://www.theguardian.com/sport/2016/sep/19/alistair-brownlee-jonny-world-triathlon-series.

Whalen, P. (1998). Fear, Vigilance and Ambiguity: Initial Neuroimaging Studies of the Human Amygdala. *Current Directions in Psychological Science*, vol. 7, no. 6, p. 177.

8 Different people's brains are wired differently

As we saw in the previous chapter, there are distinctive brain structures that explain why humans are not completely rational. We also gained an appreciation of how using different parts of the brain and body to guide decision-making offers several advantages compared to a purely rational approach. In addition, a deeper understanding of how the brain develops can suggest ways to develop more effective skills and behaviour.

Over the past twenty to thirty years we have greatly increased our knowledge of how our brains work. A major breakthrough came in the 1990s when functional magnetic resonance imaging (fMRI) scanners were used to see what was going on in our brains. This neuroimaging procedure measures brain activity by detecting changes associated with blood flow. It assumes that neurons are activated when there is blood flow in that region of the brain.

Using fMRI, researchers have made many interesting discoveries, as well as dispelling previous beliefs and myths. For example, new knowledge of how our brains are structured and work has highlighted that all humans are born with broadly similar brains and that what happens to us in our lives can cause changes in our brains. Babies are born with around 200 billion brain cells, but there are very few connections between them, particularly in the higher brain: the prefrontal cortex. The development of connections will be largely responsible for the social and emotional intelligence of the child – which parents can influence greatly. In the first few years of life, the infant brain starts to rapidly form connections. In these crucial years, connections are created, broken and recreated as a direct result of the child's experiences, particularly interactions with their parents.

Our experiences can change our brain

To illustrate this further, one fascinating piece of research scanned the brains of children from normal loving households and deprived backgrounds. The number of connections was drastically reduced for the disadvantaged children (Nelson, 2014).

Figure 8.1 reproduces the scans of two three-year-old children. The illustration on the left shows healthy child's brain whilst the one on the right

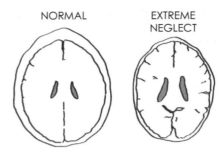

Figure 8.1 Brains of normal and extremely neglected 3-year-old children (see Tanner, C. 2017).

has been based on a scan of a Romanian orphan who suffered severe sensory deprivation. The brain on the left of the Romanian orphan was smaller and had enlarged ventricles (holes in the centre of the brain). It also showed a shrunken cortex which is the brain's outer layer.

In some extreme cases, the failure to building connections at an early age means that children are unable to walk. The overall lesson is that our early experiences have a significant impact on whether we will thrive or fail in later life.

There are some very interesting implications in all this for gender. It had long been believed that men and women had different brains, yet some innovative research published in 2015 showed that that it is impossible to tell the sex of an individual based solely on MRI scans. The research led by Daphna Joel found few structural differences between male and female brains (Joel, 2015). From her (and her colleagues') research, they found that the range was 0–8% of brains scanned contained 'all-male' or 'all-female' structures. The conclusion was that there is no such thing as a male brain or a female brain.

However, whilst they are not structural, there *are* some discernible differences between men's and women's brains. A 2016 study confirmed that the connections – or 'wiring' – of the brain go a long way to explaining why men and women behave differently. For example, in the areas that control language and speech, Dr Sandra Witelson found there is more generalised interconnectivity in the female brain than in the male brain. Women are thought to speak about 20,000 words a day on average, which is about 13,000 more than the average man.

The research in this area is fascinating and still in its very early stages. However, what is already clear that it is the wiring of the hundreds of billions of neurons in the adult brain and the way neural networks develop that determine how we behave and what our identity might be.

Analytical or creative?

A lot of people refer to being right- or left-brain dominant and how they think and process information accordingly (Figure 8.2).

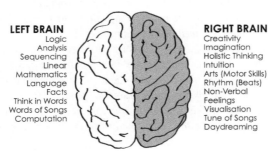

LEFT BRAIN
Logic
Analysis
Sequencing
Linear
Mathematics
Language
Facts
Think in Words
Words of Songs
Computation

RIGHT BRAIN
Creativity
Imagination
Holistic Thinking
Intuition
Arts (Motor Skills)
Rhythm (Beats)
Non-Verbal
Feelings
Visualisation
Tune of Songs
Daydreaming

Figure 8.2 Basic characteristics of left and right brain.

When people look at the above diagram, they tend to pigeonhole them-selves into one or other. But in reality, whilst they may have a natural ten-dency towards one way of thinking, the two sides of their brains typically work together in their everyday lives.

We can show different people a picture, perhaps a landscape scene. If they are asked to look at it for a few minutes and then to describe it, how they recall it will give some indication of how they might think. Did they see the overall picture and what it might mean, or did they respond to the detail?

The right brain will focus first on the whole picture and then the details, processing information in an intuitive and simultaneous way. The left brain will attempt to verbalise what it sees, processing information in an analytical and sequential way – looking at the pieces before putting them together to get the whole. Left-brain thinking is verbal and analytical. Right-brain thinking is typically non-verbal and intuitive, using pictures rather than words.

One example of this is when people give directions. The right-brain person will say something like this: 'Turn left [pointing to the left] by the park over there [pointing again]. Then you will pass a white house. Keep walking and then you will see a thatched house. At the next lights, turn right towards the church.' The left-brain person will say something like: 'From here, go west past five roads and turn south into Ash Street. Go three or four miles and then turn east onto Chancery Lane'.

The right brain is often regarded as more 'creative', while the left brain is considered more analytical. Neither is right or wrong – or better than the other. The important thing is to be aware that there are different ways of thinking and, by knowing your natural preference, you can pay attention to improving your less dominant side. Think of it in terms of wiring: you are developing new connections to access a different part of the brain. Even more interesting, although our experiences have wired our brain as it is currently, we can effectively rewire it. There is lots of evidence showing that our brains are 'plastic'.

One of the most well-known pieces of research was undertaken with London's black cab drivers. Before the days of Uber and satnavs, every taxi driver in central London had to have 'the knowledge': a detailed mental map of the capital, including about 25,000 streets and thousands of landmarks. As you can imagine, it's difficult to learn all of this and the process can take three to four years to complete. There is a final test, which often takes twelve attempts to pass. So difficult is the process that only about half of the trainee cabbies do really well in the exam.

An article published in the journal Current Biology *revealed that memorising the vast array of streets causes structural changes in the brain, including a greater volume of nerve cells in the hippocampus. Eleanor Maguire and Katherine Woollett, from the neuroimaging centre at University College London, made MRI scans of the brains of seventy-nine trainee taxi drivers and thirty-one control subjects (who weren't training to become taxi drivers). They also studied the performance of both groups in a range of unrelated memory tasks.*

At the start of the study, the participants showed no discernible differences in brain structure or memory. Previous studies had found that London taxi drivers typically have a large hippocampus (the part of the brain associated with memory, particularly long-term memory, and spatial navigation). But this was roughly the same across all participants at the outset.

Of the trainee group only thirty-nine passed the test and went on to qualify as registered taxi drivers. This gave the researchers an opportunity to further divide the volunteers into three groups: those who passed, those who trained but did not pass, and the control subjects who had never trained at all.

Among the trainees who passed the test, the neuroscientists observed an increase in grey matter (the nerve cells where processing takes place) in the back part of the hippocampus. There were no changes to the brain structure of those who had failed or never trained.

In the memory tasks, both the successful and failed cabbies were better than the control group at recalling London landmarks. However, in other tasks not related to the capital, such as recalling complex visual information, the control group and the trainees who failed to qualify were better than the registered taxi drivers who had 'the knowledge'.

'By following the trainee taxi drivers over time as they acquired — or failed to acquire — "the knowledge", we have seen directly and within individuals how the structure of the hippocampus can change with external stimulation', said Maguire in a press release. 'The human brain remains "plastic" even in adult life, allowing it to adapt when we learn new tasks.'

The famous study of London taxi drivers is just one among many that have found the brain to be capable of setting up new pathways and connections.

This is also the ethos of Stanford University psychology professor, Carol Dweck (Dweck, 2006). In her book *Mindset*, based on decades of research into achievement, Dweck claims that success is determined by whether people have a 'fixed' or 'growth' mindset. A fixed mindset is characterised by the belief that individual traits, such as intelligence and creativity, are innate and cannot be changed. A growth mindset is defined by the belief that traits are not fixed and pre-determined but constantly change and develop, According to Dweck, those with a growth mindset are likely to be more successful. Furthermore, anyone can develop a growth mindset.

If you really want to develop a new skill, such as great empathic influencing, all you have to do is change your 'wiring'. As the great Canadian psychologist, Donald Hebb, once said, 'Cells that fire together, wire together' (Hebb, 1949). Forming new habits can change the wiring in your brain.

Well, thank you, Mum and Dad!

Researchers at Cambridge University have just published a major study showing that only about 10% of the variation between people's empathy is down to their genes, and that upbringing and environment are far greater influences (Figure 8.3).

They also found (in line with other previous studies) that women are more likely to be empathic. However, this was again not genetically determined. The research further confirms that we are not 'born' empathic – it is not an inherent trait (Warrier et al., 2018). Therefore, we can change the wiring of our brains, as described in this chapter, which means that we can develop our empathic influencing skills.

If you believe that empathic influencing can make the difference in your life, you will need to create new pathways by just doing it. Adopt new behaviours and repeat them to create a habit – and then new wiring in your brain.

Can people really change? It's a question I am frequently asked as a coach. My answer, based on experience of working with many leaders, is a resounding 'yes'. However, I would add that the leader has to really want to change and must be prepared to put the time and effort in.

Simon was an IT director in a large pharmaceutical organisation. He was respected for his expertise and technical knowledge and had been promoted to the board. He had worked in the organisation for ten years and over that time had built good relationships with his fellow board members and chief executive. He was keen on rugby – and other pursuits that might be considered typically male – and connected with – mainly male – colleagues by attending such events. On the whole, life at work was pretty comfortable.

Figure 8.3 Influence of upbringing.

However, there were some rumblings from his staff that, while he had a clear and direct vision, he was too autocratic. Some of his behaviour, they said, was so directive some felt it bordered on bullying and certain staff members, particularly women, did not feel comfortable with him.

When we first started working together, he acknowledged some of these issues. However, what concerned him greatly were the changes at board level. The chief executive had retired and three of his fellow directors had also moved on. With the 'new guard' in, he felt isolated and unsupported. Furthermore, he recognised he needed to change his default leadership style.

The goal of the coaching was to help him develop those relationships and in turn his leadership of his staff. We undertook an emotional intelligence assessment and also identified what his emotional drivers were. The findings suggested that Simon had clear emotional intelligence strengths: he was highly assertive, independently minded, flexible and capable of coping with stress. However, he scored considerably lower on impulse control, empathy, interpersonal relationships and emotional expression. The results completely reflected what he was struggling with at this time: the need to build new relationships and a team who were having issues with a leadership style that was direct and 'shot from the hip', with little thought about the impact of his words.

The crux was to work on building Simon's empathy and interpersonal relationships. Over the course of the following sessions he showed signs of greater empathy and also started to work on ways of connecting more deeply with people. He found ways of building rapport with his board colleagues and made similar connections within his team. He became very aware of the impact that he had on others and thought more carefully about what he said – and how he said it. People started to notice a big change in him, as he became more interested in them. As time went on Simon's behaviour changed further. He became a more rounded leader and ended up joining another organisation as their global Vice President for Technology. Part of his success in the selection process was down to recent examples of engaging with people and influencing them, as great empathic influencing was a key requirement in this new role.

Clearly Simon had set up new pathways in his brain in order to behave differently. And by continually working on this rewiring process, he succeeded in embedding a totally new management style and reaching new career heights.

Summary of key points

- There are few structural differences between people's brains. It is their experiences that generate the connections within the organ and create discernible differences.
- The connections (or wiring) are not fixed and we can change them.
- There is evidence that demonstrates our brains change through learning.
- Mindset is key – and a growth mindset can lead to achievement and success.
- Empathic influencing is a skill that can be developed by creating new 'wiring'.

References

Dweck, C. (2006). *Mindset, How You Can Fulfil Your Potential*. New York: Random House.

Hebb, D. O. (1949). *The Organisation of Behaviour*. New York: Wiley.

Joel, D. (2015, December). Sex beyond Genitalia: The Human Brain Mosaic. *Proceedings of the National Academies of Sciences*, vol. 112, no. 50, pp. 15468–15473.

Nelson, C. A., Gox, N. A. and Zeanah, C. H. (2014). *Romania's Abandoned Children: Deprivation, Brain Development and the Struggle for Recovery*. Cambridge, MA and London: Harvard University Press.

Tanner, C. (2017). A Tale of Two Toddler Brain Scans: One Shows the Shocking Impact Caused by Abuse and the Other Reveals the Difference Love Can Make – But Can You Tell Which Is Which? *Mailonline*.

Warrier,V., Toro, R., Chakrabarti, B., theiPSYCH-Broadautismgroup, Børglum, A., Grove, J., the 23andMe Research Team, Hinds, D.A., Bourgeron, T., Baron-Cohen, S., (2018). Genome-Wide Analyses of Self-reported Empathy: Correlations with Autism, Schizophrenia, and Anorexia Nervosa. *Translational Psychiatry*, vol. 8, no. 1, pp. 35. doi:10.1038/s41398-017-0082-6

Woolett, K. and Maguire, E. A. (2011). Acquiring 'the Knowledge' of London's Layout Drives Structural Brain Changes. *Current Biology*, vol. 21, pp. 2109–2114.

Part IV

You DARE!

9 To develop empathic influencing you first need to understand it

As we have seen, empathic influencing is a core skill for success in both your professional and personal life. But to develop it you need to understand it fully.

Let's sum up what we've established so far. Empathic influencing is the ability to understand your own and others' perspectives. To have exceptional self-awareness and to know exactly what you are thinking and feeling. To be able to see something from others' perspectives almost as closely as they see it themselves. To be able to communicate, present information and interact at every level with an excellent appreciation of what resonates positively with other people. To do all this with the positive intention of connecting and communicating successfully, honouring the other person's perspective.

The fundamentals of empathic influencing have a basis in what we traditionally think of as empathy, but with the added dimension of influencing action to result in a positive outcome for everyone involved.

To develop this idea further, we first need to be clear on what exactly empathy is. The *Oxford Dictionary* definition for empathy is as follows:

> The ability to understand and share the feelings of another.

To expand that further and to be more precise about how the importance of how others truly see the world, the following definition from Wikipedia captures this.

> *Empathy* is the capacity to understand or feel what another person is experiencing from within the other being's frame of reference, i.e., the capacity to place oneself in another's position. Empathy is seeing with the eyes of another, listening with the ears of another and feeling with the heart of another.

What is interesting about this definition is that whilst empathy enables us to understand or feel another person's perspective, it does not mean that we will behave differently. I have worked with some people who are excellent at reading the feelings of other people and yet they just do not demonstrate their

Figure 9.1 Cognitive empathy.

insights through their actions. They 'know' but they aren't doing anything with that knowledge.

If we delve a little deeper into the research on empathy, we find a partial explanation for this. Psychologists classify empathy into three types: cognitive, emotional and somatic.

Cognitive empathy is all about understanding another's thoughts and emotions in a very rational, logical way. It is seeing someone else's perspective but not engaging in any feelings about those perspectives. Cognitive empathy can be very useful for people involved in negotiations of any sort. It can also be very dangerous. As Daniel Goleman in 2017 points out in his blog, torturers need good cognitive empathy to know how best to hurt someone. For them it would be a disadvantage to have any feelings or sympathy for their victim. Whilst torturers are an extreme example, there are many ordinary people, especially leaders, who exhibit the same tendencies (see Chapter 6 on the dark side of empathic influencing) (Figure 9.1).

Emotional empathy (sometimes referred to as affective empathy) is when you intuitively feel what another person is feeling. It is sometimes described as emotional 'contagion', because it's almost as if you 'catch' the emotion, in the same way as you might catch a cold. Affective empathy can be subdivided into the following categories:

- *Empathic concern* – sympathy and compassion for others in response to their suffering
- *Personal distress* – self-centred feelings of discomfort and anxiety in response to another's suffering. This is the first type of empathy that we experience and has been observed in children just 18 months old (Figure 9.2).

Figure 9.2 Emotional empathy.

Somatic empathy is a physical reaction, probably based on the responses of mirror neurons in the somatic nervous system (the part of the nervous system associated with voluntary muscular movements). For example, our heart might race when we are watching a frightening film or we might smile (sometimes unknowingly), when we see something that is funny. It is quite fascinating to observe people watching TV, as their eyes light up or they spontaneously smile at scenes on their screens. Some people even cry when they see someone else crying (Figure 9.3).

To develop empathic influencing skills, we need to engage all three types of empathy. We need to feel what the other person is feeling, we need to be aware of our own physical and emotional reactions and then we need to see their perspective rationally – without being consumed by the feelings. Finally, we need to deploy good problem-solving skills to decide how best to approach the person and the situation.

Figure 9.3 Somatic empathy.

Eric was out running one early evening. The weather was lovely and he wanted to catch the last few minutes before darkness fell. At one point, he decided to take a narrow path. In the distance he could see two people and a very large dog. As he came closer, the dog started to run at him. It was barking, growling and snarling. It seemed to Eric that any moment it would bite his legs. And that made him angry. Why couldn't he go for a peaceful run without getting attacked by a dog? He remonstrated with the two walkers. He aggressively shouted that they should have their dog under control. An argument ensued, as they pointed out that he had just appeared out of nowhere and what did he expect? The dog was protecting them.

Eric stopped, managed his impulses and reflected on the situation. The walkers were two women. They had a big dog. It was getting dark. He put himself in their shoes and could see that they must have felt vulnerable, particularly in the twilight. Yes, he was cross that part of his run was spoilt but he didn't want the situation to escalate to where it was likely heading. For his part he felt anger; on their part the emotion was fear.

Understanding this, Eric dissipated the tension. He said he agreed that seeing a man looming suddenly out of the twilight could be unnerving. He showed a great understanding of their perspective. They also acknowledged that they would have put the dog on the lead, had they seen him. Both parties appreciated and understood where the other stood. The conversation ended on a positive note.

Summary of key points

- There are three types of empathy – cognitive, emotional and somatic.
- We need all three types for empathy for effective empathic influencing.

References

Oxford Dictionary. (online version 2019). Accessed: February 18, 2019. https://en.oxforddictionaries.com.

Wikipedia. (2019). Accessed: December 28, 2018. https://en.m.wikipedia.org/wiki/Empathy.

10 Developing empathic influencing skills using 'DARE'

To start to develop your empathic influencing, remember the four steps that we saw at the beginning of this book (Figure 10.1).

The first step is to assess where you are on this model. You might already have some idea of where you stand from, for example, completing an emotional intelligence assessment or eliciting feedback from your colleagues. It is always important to evaluate with honesty what you are good at and where you might need to develop. You can complete a questionnaire on the website www.trulyauthenticleaders.com to help you further.

In the meantime, the rest of this chapter provides some ideas about how to develop at each stage.

Stage 1 – Different: awareness of others as different from you

Before you can understand others, you first have to understand yourself. And to achieve radical self-awareness, you first have to appreciate the uniqueness of both your experiences and your psychological DNA. By considering how all this has made you who you are today, you will glimpse how different experiences and a different genetic make-up can create people who are very different from you.

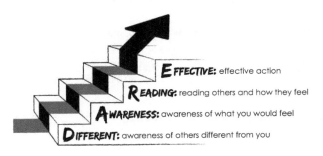

EFFECTIVE: effective action

READING: reading others and how they feel

AWARENESS: awareness of what you would feel

DIFFERENT: awareness of others different from you

Figure 10.1 Four steps to empathic influencing.

THIS IS ME!

* EMOTIONAL SELF   * INDEPENDENCE   * IMPULSE CONTROL
  AWARENESS   * PROBLEM SOLVING   * FLEXIBILITY
* SELF REGARD   * REALITY TESTING   * STRESS TOLERANCE
* SELF ACTUALISATION   * OPTIMISM

Figure 10.2 This is *me*.

In other words, although this stage is about understanding that other people are different, it starts with truly appreciating your own journey and how it has shaped you.

If we think about the emotional intelligence variables we discussed in Chapter 1, we can apply that to how we respond and react. For example, if we have high optimism, we may interpret information and events positively. With good self-regard we may believe that we can achieve most things. Our reality testing may determine how we see events, i.e. overly positive, overly negative or realistically. What is our level of self-awareness and how deep does that go? (Figure 10.2).

There are a number of techniques to deepen your self-awareness. They can all support and reinforce each other, and they combine to give a good understanding of yourself. They fall into the following categories:

* Trip down memory lane: what do you learn about yourself when you reflect on your past and experiences?
* What would others – colleagues, family or friends – say about you?
* Using psychometrics: tests and instruments designed by experts.

Some exercises to help you understand yourself

Your life story

Reflect on your life up to this point. Consider the 'highs' and 'lows'. What made them the 'highs' and what was behind the 'lows'? After reflecting on

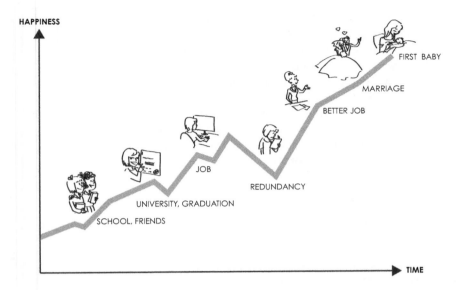

Figure 10.3 Life story.

this, either draw your own graph of life (see example above or go to the website www.trulyauthenticleaders.com for more) and/or develop a series of chapters with your key reflections (Figure 10.3).

Whether on your graph or in your chapters, do the high points in your life have any recurrent themes? For example, did they occur when you were doing things with others? Or were they more to do with your greatest achievements? If so, what have been your key accomplishments?

Here are some other questions and points for reflection:

- When you were a child (up to about the age of eleven) what did you enjoy doing? What did you want to be when you grew up? Identify the key themes that you notice from this.
- What gives you the greatest joy and what do you love doing? Identify three activities from both your personal life and your professional life? What are you passionate about and what inspires you?
- Who do you most admire and why? What is it about these people that you respect and value?
- What are your core values? For a list of values and exercises to identify them go to the website www.trulyauthenticleaders.com.

Now for some deeper stuff! Think back to your family and growing up.

- How would you describe your father?
- How would you describe your mother?

- What were (or weren't) you allowed to feel and do at home? What were the explicit rules? What were the unspoken rules?
- Do you have any siblings?
- Where are you in the birth order and any impact of that?
- What was valued in your home?
- How was conflict dealt with in your home?
- What was your father's typical advice? And your mother's?
- Were there any commonly repeated expressions in your home? Examples might be: 'Money is the root of all evil', 'Don't upset the apple cart', 'Adversity shapes character'.
- What would be your epitaph?

How others view you

Perhaps you can readily answer these questions or perhaps you really aren't sure. Ask yourself:

- How would family and friends describe me?
- What would colleagues say about me?
- What strengths and weaknesses emerge from my performance reviews?

If you don't think you know the answers, then ask! Find four to five people at work and put the following questions to them. You could even do an informal 360-degree assessment (go to www.trulyauthenticleaders.com to download a form and instructions).

- What do I do well?
- What could I do even better?
- If you were describing me to someone else, what three words would you use?

Alternatively, approach friends and family and ask the following:

- What's good about me?
- Can you spend three minutes describing me?

Now try to capture exactly what they said by writing it down.

Psychometrics

The above two exercises are very useful but can be limited by the sphere you operate in. For example, if you consider yourself from the perspective of your peer group, you are limited by the typical behaviour and norms of that group. If your friends are all highly extrovert, you might see yourself as an introvert. Yet in comparison to the general population you could be averagely extrovert. A well-validated and reliable psychometric assessment will give you a view of your position in the wider world. It can give you an objective perspective on what your strongest characteristics are.

Many psychometric assessments are available. Your choice will depend on exactly what you want to measure. You could look, for instance, at the well-known Sixteen Personality Factor Questionnaire (16PF) (see www.16fpf. com), which uses the descriptors below. You can go to the website www. trulyauthenticleaders.com to find out more. If you have already taken it, did it support your assumptions? Or were there some surprises?

Warmth – the extent to which one will become warmly involved with others.
Reasoning – abstract thinker.
Emotional stability – extent to which one can cope with the daily demands of life.
Dominance – extent to which one attempts to exert influence over other.
Liveliness – spontaneity of expression and excitement seeking.
Rule consciousness – extent to which external rules and/or standards are valued and followed.
Social boldness – extent to which one has ease in social situations.
Sensitivity – extent to which subjective feelings influences judgement on issues.
Vigilance – the likelihood of questioning the motives behind the words and actions of others.
Abstractedness – the extent to which you attend to practical, concrete aspects of the environment or the thought processes they trigger and your imagination.
Privacy – extent to which one like to keep personal information private.
Apprehension – extent to which one is self-critical and apprehensive.
Openness to change – the extent to which one is open to new ideas and experiences.
Self-reliant – extent to which one is self-reliant, solitary and self-sufficient or be around people and involved in group activities.
Perfectionism – extent to which it is important to behave in line with clearly defined personal standards and being organised.
Tension – the extent of physical tension expressed by impatience and irritability with others.

Another psychometric assessment that I have found particularly useful is Management Research Group's Individual Directions Inventory (see www. MRG.com). Its creators describe it as follows:

> *The Individual Directions Inventory (IDI) is a tool for personal and professional development that provides you with the opportunity to explore your motivations and preferences, examine how these have affected the choices you have made in different areas of your life and consider what actions you might wish to take as you look toward your future. The IDI provides information about areas from which*

you are presently gaining satisfaction, as well as identifying areas which you may find less appealing. By helping you understand the types of settings, roles and approaches that may hold the greatest interest for you, the IDI can be a useful tool in helping you to orient yourself in both your personal and professional worlds.

The tool has been validated by psychologists and is great for understanding your own emotional drivers and really deepening your self-awareness. It is particularly useful in identifying factors that are hard wired into you and don't change greatly over time.

It is also useful as a framework to start considering other people's motivations and drivers (and can be used in a team setting). This is invaluable when we are at level 3 of the DARE model.

The drivers or directions are described as follows:

Affiliating

Giving: Gaining satisfaction from relating to others by providing them with support, affection and empathy.

Receiving: Gaining satisfaction from relating to others in order to receive support, affection and empathy from them.

Belonging: Gaining satisfaction from relating to others by developing mutual bonds of loyalty, cooperation and friendship.

Expressing: Gaining satisfaction from relating to others by expressing oneself in a direct, spontaneous and emotionally uninhibited manner.

Attracting

Gaining Stature: Gaining satisfaction from obtaining social rewards such as recognition, status and respect as the result of social skills, achievements and/or activities.

Entertaining: Gaining satisfaction from obtaining social rewards such as admiration and visibility by using personal charisma and talent to enliven situations and entertain people.

Perceiving

Creating: Gaining satisfaction from being imaginative and original and perceiving one's world in an innovative and creative manner.

Interpreting: Gaining satisfaction from seeking intellectual stimulation and perceiving one's world in a logical, analytical and non-emotional manner.

Mastering

Excelling: Gaining satisfaction from challenging oneself and pushing for ever-higher levels of achievement.

Enduring: Gaining satisfaction from demonstrating persistence, determination and tenacity.

Structuring: Gaining satisfaction from controlling one's environment through the use of organisation, precision and thoroughness.

Challenging

Manoeuvring: Gaining satisfaction from actively seeking and pursuing opportunities in the environment and turning them to one's advantage.

Winning: Gaining satisfaction from acting in a forceful, aggressive and directly competitive manner in order to win.

Controlling: Gaining satisfaction from being in charge, having power and authority, influencing and controlling people and events.

Maintaining

Stability: Gaining satisfaction from minimising risk by maintaining a predictable, safe and consistent environment.

Independence: Gaining satisfaction from being self-reliant and staying free of external controls on personal autonomy.

Irreproachability: Gaining satisfaction from ascribing to and striving towards ideal behaviour and a personal code, which places one beyond reproach.

By bringing together the results of the three types of exercises above, you should be in a great position to recognise consistent themes and to fully understand who you are. You could consolidate what you have discovered by writing a paragraph to describe the 'real' you.

Beginning to understand others

As you can see from the exercises described above, the person you are is a combination of many factors. It follows that, with a different set of experiences and personality traits, you would come up with a different final paragraph. This enables you to start thinking about the paragraphs that other people might write about themselves.

I had a conversation with one client about his holiday. He had had a fantastic time and told me of all the things he had done in just a short time. He had clearly planned the holiday well. I thought that perhaps he had found an excellent guidebook. As I probed a little deeper, I discovered that he had consulted some friends who had visited the same country. He explained that they had shared their Excel spreadsheets of what to do. He then used that information to develop his own spreadsheet for the trip. I was fascinated by such a planned approach. He was incredulous that I didn't organise my holidays in the same way. Didn't everybody use an Excel spreadsheet?

This is a typical example of how different people are. My client and his peer group would always use a planned, methodical and detailed approach. My attitude is somewhat more spontaneous. There are many other everyday examples of how human beings differ from one another. Just try discussing the following with friends or colleagues:

- How do you/they choose a birthday present for a loved one?
- How do you/they respond to good news?
- How do you/they respond to bad news?

Every single day, you'll find countless examples of difference if you look for them. You can also use some of the frameworks and questions from the section on understanding yourself above to think about how A.N. Other might be different from you. When I coach people about how to influence others, whether boss, peers or direct reports, I ask my clients to write a pen portrait of somebody else, based on the ideas outlined above. I get them to think hard about why these colleagues come to work (taking money out of the equation). Do they like working with people? Are they motivated by status? Do they like to achieve? If my clients don't know, I get them to try and find out by engaging and talking more to the people they chose to describe.

- How do they spend their spare time?
- What do they value?
- What do they enjoy?

This exercise is essential for learning how to influence people in your network, but it's also useful for developing your appreciation of difference. Ideally you would choose someone outside your usual circle of friends to write about, especially if they're all a bit like you. For example, I asked the client who used Excel to plan his holiday to describe how someone who didn't need a spreadsheet would have a good time!

You can also challenge yourself to talk to a wider range of people than normal. Ask questions with genuine curiosity. Listen with no judgement. Understand and appreciate how they might see the world. Your aim is just to appreciate difference.

Based on the perceptual positioning exercise from neuro-linguistic programming (NLP; Bateson, 1972; John Grinder et al., 1975) there is another good exercise to think about someone who you want to influence. Position three imaginary chairs facing each other. Position one is you, position two is the person you want to influence and position three is an observer, maybe a coach (Figure 10.4).

Sit in an imaginary chair one and say what you want to say to the person in position two. What are you saying? What are your assumptions? You are seeing, feeling and hearing the situation through your own filters.

Move to imaginary chair two and adopt the stance of being the person you want to influence. How would they respond to what you have said? What might they ask? How would they disagree with you? What are they thinking and feeling after what you said? How will they show or express it? Try to see, feel and hear the situation through the filters of the other person.

Now move to position three. You are the observer and sage! What have you heard from both perspectives? What would you advise as a result from hearing both sides of the story? This time, you are seeing, feeling and hearing the situation through the filters of an observer.

Are you at the point where you can see that people are just very different to you?

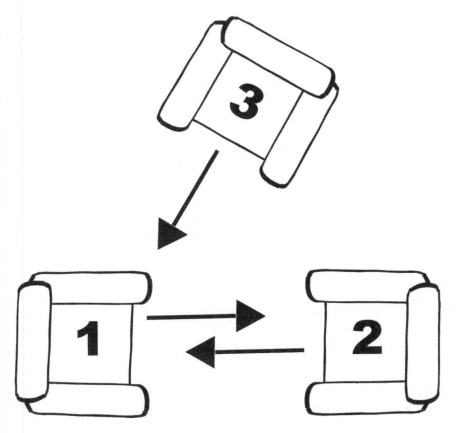

Figure 10.4 Perceptual positioning.

Stage 2 – Awareness of self: how would I feel?

At stage 2, you are thinking about yourself again. How would you feel and/or think receiving your own message? However, you are probably asking yourself this question when you're planning a difficult conversation with someone else or reviewing a discussion that didn't go well. Perhaps you're even thinking this way during a tricky conversation!

Janet is a confident and ambitious woman. She wants to motivate her direct report, Gail, to take the next step in her career. She tells her that 'with a little more effort she will be promoted rapidly and will be single-handedly leading the division'. Janet knows that if her boss had said that to her when she was more junior, she would have felt inspired and energised to take the next step. Gail loves her job and working with her team. She also loves stability and at this stage she doesn't want to move. Janet's comment to her made her feel unsafe and a little fearful.

Very often people at stage 2 have some empathic recognition that others may react strongly to what they say or do. However, the range of reactions they expect are limited by their own experiences. There's nothing wrong with this! In fact, it's essential to go through this stage. By understanding how you would react you deepen your own self-awareness and prepare for stage 3, where you will start to understand how others would react.

After the exercises in stage 1, you should understand yourself reasonably well. This stage involves going little bit further and thinking about *how you react* to other people and situations.

This stage is about a stimulus or input, such as a comment or an action, and the response to it. It is fascinating to observe how people react differently to the same message. Clearly the reaction depends on how they have interpreted the message internally, as well as the message itself.

I challenge my clients to reflect with deep awareness so that they understand what might make them react in a less than objective way.

A few years ago, I was coaching an MD who had an issue with his temper. The impact of losing his temper with people was, as you can imagine, quite negative for himself personally and his business. When we explored the *issue* further, we found that he lost *his* temper when he perceived that *there were doubts about him* 'being good enough'. I use the word 'perceived', as the *doubts were* what he heard, but the reality was that *they were never openly expressed*. When he construed *that someone had questioned* his capability, he *inevitably* turned angry. It was *as* if the comment and his reaction were *welded* together. *Clearly, he needed to apply some impulse control, so that he could choose a more appropriate response and engage his more rational brain* (Figure 10.5).

To develop deeper self-awareness, it is a good idea to reflect on experiences that have triggered strong reactions in some way – positively or negatively. They will usually relate to something that happened in your childhood. The aim of this part of the book is not to discover *why* you are provoked, but to understand *what* you are sensitive about, so that you can deal with such situations more effectively.

Try the following exercise:

- Think of a situation or conversation that you reacted strongly to.
- What was the impact on you? How did you react?
- Can you reconstruct your inner dialogue?
- Do you have a more rational and objective assessment now?
- What lessons will you take into the future?

Here's a real-life example to help you.

My client, Jill, was a director of operations. Her boss had asked her to think of some ideas to enhance her team's efficiency. The next time they met, he came to her with an idea for her team that the finance director had come up with.

Jill felt that she had been undermined. In her words, 'It was like asking your dentist how to operate on your leg.' The experience knocked her confidence and her motivation. She felt angry and frustrated with her boss.

STIMULUS   DEFAULT RESPONSE

STIMULUS   1. IMPULSE CONTROL TO IDENTIFY
                     YOUR CHOICE OF REPONSE

                  2. CHOOSE THE MOST APPROPRIATE
                     RESPONSE FOR THE OUTCOME YOU
                     WANT

Figure 10.5 Choosing the most appropriate response for the outcome you want.

The thoughts going through her head *at the time* were: *'Does he not realise that I know my stuff'? 'Am I not doing a good enough job'? 'Maybe everyone will find out that I can't do my job properly'? 'What will my peers think of me'?*

She then started to apply her more rational brain: 'He always seeks opinion far and wide.' 'He frequently asks me for my views on financial matters and other areas outside my remit'. 'This is typical behaviour from him'. 'He is trying to stimulate different thinking'. 'He has told me he thinks I am great at my job'.

Eventually, Jill came to the following conclusions: 'I know I am good at my job and I don't need to react defensively'. 'When I look at the things that make me unhappy and distress me, they usually have something to do with lack of confidence'. 'If I really believe deep down that I am good at my job, I won't react negatively to these situations in the future'.

Jill's story illustrates how limiting first reactions can be – and the power of applying a more rational perspective. It also shows how a different 'self-talk' or inner dialogue may produce a completely different response from the same person.

Now, think of remarks of your own that have yielded a strong reaction from others. If you were on the receiving end, what would you feel and think – and how would you react? You might think the comment was quite innocuous. Or in a certain situation with a particular inner dialogue, it might hit a raw nerve.

One of my clients was at an event that was being delivered by two people: a man and a woman. There was an obvious rapport between the two presenters. As the second day was drawing to a close, my client made what she thought was a slightly mischievous comment about the sexual tension between the presenters. The response was extreme. The female walked out and refused to take part in the rest of the programme. My client had no idea what she had triggered.

As you replay meetings you have attended, conversations you have had or arguments you have witnessed, ask yourself what you would think and feel, if that was said to you. Then think through what actually happened and how that compares.

Stage 3 – Reading others: how do they feel?

In stage 2, I hope you started to develop a deeper understanding of how you might feel in certain situations. That is a highly valuable skill in itself. But now you need to understand the dynamic of bringing someone else into the mix.

Think of all that is going on within you. So it is for other people. Your challenge is to work out what might be going on within them. You need to try and understand what will make them react both positively and negatively. So how do you go about it?

For people you are in contact with regularly, there are a number of techniques, including the following. Whilst your assessment may be based on generalisations, it is at least a starting point to identify and test hypotheses.

Give others high-quality attention

Just talk to other people and really listen! Don't just listen to their words. Listen to their tone and look at their body language when they are talking. In some of my workshops, I run exercises where I ask participants to pay high levels of attention to each other. I ask them to listen for three minutes at that level, before changing places and being listened to. Invariably, the feedback is that both parties started to understand the other person at a deeper level. Just think what we could all learn, if we applied that level of attention and listening in our daily lives.

It has been suggested that our minds wander about 50% of the time. This is very natural, but while our minds are wandering, we are not really paying attention to the person we are with. If we can remain focused on what someone is saying to us, rather than our next meeting or what we might be having for dinner, we will learn a great deal more. We will begin to grasp what is important to other people and get a sense of their values.

Observe others

By simply observing others, we can learn a great deal. A great exercise I have given to coaching clients is to go and spend time in a public place – just watching interactions. They are not allowed to get close enough to hear the conversation, but they have to guess from the body language what exactly is going on. They find that, even with complete strangers, they can make a good guess about what was being said.

So often we ignore the information we get from body language. If you can consciously develop the skill of seeing what people are thinking, feeling or saying, it will become second nature when you are interacting with others and 'distracted' by their words. You will start to notice when people are more interested and engaged. You will also see when they aren't. You will identify what is different with different interactions and possibly even start to identify what might upset or please others.

Find out about interests and hobbies

Enquire about other people's interests and hobbies. What might that tell you about them? Do they like team sports or prefer more solitary activities? Is their idea of a great evening spending time with their family or a riotous night out with friends? What do they do on holiday? Is it a relaxing week on the beach, a spa break or a high-octane adventure holiday? There are so many clues as to what a person is really like in their chosen interests and hobbies.

Look through the keyhole!

In essence this is looking at someone's environment and the choices they have made about it. The environment could be their home, their office or their car. Are they a neatness freak or is there some disorder? Do they have many photos? If so, are they of family or activities? A great book to help with this is Sam Gosling's *Snoop: What Your Stuff Says About You*.

You may also be able to draw conclusions from how someone dresses. Are they traditional or conservative? Do they conform to the company culture? There are lots of little give-aways about what people think is important in their appearance.

Certainly, it is easier to look through the keyhole at people you have met more than once, but if you practise, you may be able to find out a great deal about someone you have only just been introduced to.

Identify the Achilles heel

As you now know, you have a rich inner dialogue, a selection of limiting beliefs and a portfolio of experiences that together create a (sometimes unhelpful) response to stimuli. So too does the person you are speaking to. Just look at the way people provoke each other in meetings! Someone makes you feel 'not good enough', so you go on the attack. He comes back with a stronger comment and so the conversation spirals downwards (Figure 10.6).

Figure 10.6 Working with others.

Figure 10.7 Making ethical choices with other's Achilles heel.

However, if you can identify the other person's Achilles heel, you can have great communication. Remember the illustration below that we also showed in Chapter 6. The key here is not to stab at the weak point but to avoid prodding it! (Figure 10.7).

Meanwhile back in the real world...

Reading others in everyday life is just a step on from all the exercises above. It is about seeing the world as they see the world – and what that means for them. It also means reflecting on your own experiences. How and when have you noticed others overreacting? Are there consistent themes?

I frequently work with teams whose objective is to build trust. In several cases I have used an exercise where each member of the team undertakes some self-disclosure. The rest of the team has to listen attentively and ask themselves how it might feel to be that person. Occasionally the person who is self-disclosing explains what the impact has been on their life. For example, one woman talked about being brought up in poverty with an alcoholic father. She revealed that her highly assertive manner was a result of learning from an early age that she had to stand up for herself. In meetings it was clear that she would always respond to the slightest hint that others were 'bullying her' (even if they weren't). Another man talked about witnessing his mother being physically abused and that he was always highly motivated to stand up for the weaker members of the team.

You may not be able to do this exercise with your own team but using the perceptual positioning activity we described earlier in this chapter will help you to step into your colleagues' shoes.

Stage 4 – Effective action: using your newfound insights

This stage involves taking all the information from the previous three stages and deciding how you will act on it. After completing each of the previous stages successfully, you will know yourself well and understand what makes you react in a certain way. You will also be getting more adept at reading other people. You should now have a good sense of what will 'land well' with them and how they will react. In addition, you should have a good idea about how to present information to get the best response. Finally, you can see how useful your newfound knowledge will be for any form of communication, whether a presentation, discussion paper or response to an email. Here is a checklist you can use to ensure that you communicate in an empathic influencing style:

1   What are my key messages – what do I want to say in an unfiltered way?
2   Who is my audience and how will it like to hear this information?
3   How do I give my key messages in a way that will resonate with them?
4   Imagine listening to it now with their ears or (if it's a written communication) reading it with their eyes. How could it be misinterpreted? What needs to be refined?

The above checklist is all very well if you have time to plan and develop your communication. However, you will often have to respond in the moment. The following is an exercise to help with such situations.

You are in a dynamic situation, where you know how you feel and in the moment you can see you are reacting (whether you show it or not). You can also see that the other person is reacting too. Try to visualise what is happening as if you were in a helicopter above. With this distance, you may see that you are falling into a vicious circle and a downward spiral in the conversation. You can now make choices about what you want to do.

One tactic is to 'name the process'. Detach yourself from the content of the conversation and describe the process that you are observing: 'We just seem to be going in circles'; 'We both seem to be getting upset'; or whatever it is that you see. Then you can either move the conversation on to a more productive footing or agree to leave it until you are both calmer.

Another very simple technique is to clarify your intentions. In his book *The Speed of Trust*, Stephen Covey states: 'We judge others by their behaviour and ourselves by our intentions.' The downside of this fact is that we inevitably make erroneous assumptions about others' behaviour. One obvious solution is to close the gap between your intentions and any possible misinterpretation of your behaviour by clearly stating what your objectives are. For example, if you are going to give feedback to your direct reports, what is your intention? It is usually to enable them to be the best they can be. However, unless you tell them so upfront, they might hear instead that you don't rate them or want to score points. If they know that your intentions are positive, they can judge your behaviour in a more accurate way (Figure 10.8).

Figure 10.8 Taking the helicopter view.

Throughout this book I have talked about how empathic influencing can help you in various situations. For more ideas about how to develop your skills, visit our website www.trulyauthenticleaders.com, which includes explanations for using the DARE model in specific contexts, such as:

- Better networking.
- Better teamworking.
- Developing your image and exposure.
- Avoiding unconscious bias.
- Developing your authentic leadership.
- Making authentic choices.
- Listening to your intuition.

Summary of key points

- Use the DARE model to understand where you are and where you need to develop.
- Develop yourself at stage 1 with your own individual 'memory lane' exercises, feedback from others and psychometrics.
- Develop yourself at stage 2 by thinking about how others might have answered your questions in stage 1, developing a pen portrait with some key questions and perspective-taking.
- Develop yourself at stage 3 by giving others deep and high-quality attention, observing them closely, finding out about their interests and hobbies, noticing their physical environment, and understanding what 'triggers' them.
- Develop yourself at stage 4 by acting on your new knowledge and doing so in a structured way, such as taking the 'helicopter' view and naming the process or stating your intentions.

References

Bateson, G. (1972). *Steps to an Ecology of Mind.* Chicago and London: University of Chicago Press.
Covey, S. M. R. (2006). *The Speed of Trust.* London: Simon & Schuster.
Gosling, S. (2009). *Snoop.* London: Profile Books.
Grinder, J., Bandler R. and Delozier, J. (1975). *Patterns of Hypnotic Techniques of Milton H. Erikson, M.D.* vol. 2. Cupertino, CA: Meta Publications.

Part V
Final thoughts

11 A Utopian world where everyone trusts everyone else

At the heart of everything – and I mean everything – is trust. Trust is the bedrock for great relationships, happiness in life and success at work, whether as a leader or team member.

When you work in a low-trust environment, there are significant costs – both tangible and intangible. People find it stressful, as they are always trying to second-guess the motives of others and they believe that no one else's intentions are 'honourable'. So much energy is wasted on all this and the situation can easily spiral into negativity. Furthermore, by using the DARE model, you can see how behaviours are incorrectly attributed to perceived negative intentions.

When there is low trust, a significant amount of time is spent on double-checking information and verifying promises. When you really trust people you know that, if they say they will do something by a certain time, then it's effectively already done. You can rely on them and use your time for better things than following up. If you count up the hours you spend in a day, week or year dealing with issues related to low trust, you will begin to measure its true cost. For example, it has been proven that trust can reduce the transaction costs of investment decisions (Covey, 2006).

With trusting relationships you know that the agenda and intentions of others are positive. They may say things to you that are challenging, but in an environment of trust you accept the challenge and value it. This enables you to grow and develop.

Trust increases certainty, which – you may recall – is something that our brain values. We become surer of how others will behave and are not driven to respond based on the fear of unpredictability. This means that we can say our piece (albeit within the DARE model) and move things forward, knowing that others will behave consistently and in our best interests (Figure 11.1).

The research into trust is fascinating and adds so much to our DARE model. One expert is the American neuroeconomist, Paul Zak, who has done many interesting studies on trust and its implications. In an early project (Zak, 2012), he built economic models of what makes countries prosper. He found that the most important factor in the success of a society and the

Figure 11.1 Trust is the bedrock.

development of its economy was not natural resources, education, healthcare or work ethic but trustworthiness. Alas, this important finding seems to be largely ignored by governments throughout the world.

Zak has done further work and established that showing others that you trust them triggers the release of oxytocin, which makes us feel more generous, caring and good about ourselves. In addition, when people feel trusted, they become more trustworthy, creating a virtuous circle. Zak claims that trust explains

> why some people give freely of themselves and others are cold-hearted bastards, why some people cheat and steal and others you can trust with your life, why some husbands are more faithful than others and why women tend to be more generous – and nicer – than men.
>
> (his words not mine!)

Furthermore, in a series of experiments Zak has also shown that oxytocin makes us feel empathy for others. In fact, he has described it as the 'biological substrate for empathy', connecting us emotionally to others and making us help strangers, as well as people we know (Zak, 2014). Interestingly he has also found that extreme stress releases epinephrine, which inhibits the production of oxytocin. Think of all those organisations with many burnt out people and their inability to be empathic to others!

Zak's more recent research (Zak, 2017) has looked at organisations and the findings are compelling. He has found that employees in high-trust environments:

- Are more productive.
- Have more energy at work.
- Collaborate better with colleagues.
- Stay with their employers longer.
- Have less chronic stress.
- Are happier with their lives.
- Which all lead to a superior performance.

He also found that those who experience both higher trust and purpose at work release even more oxytocin and experience even higher joy. What's more, his recent research in the United States found that, compared to people in low-trust organisations, people in high-trust organisations:

- Had 106% more energy.
- Were 76% more engaged.
- Were 50% more productive.
- Showed greater loyalty – with 88% ready to recommend their employer to family and friends.

Better still:

- 60% enjoyed their work more.
- 70% were more aligned with their company's purpose.
- 66% felt closer to their colleagues.
- 11% had more empathy for their work mates and depersonalised them 41% less.
- 40% suffered less burnout from their work.
- 41% had a greater sense of accomplishment.
- The employees earned 17% more.

This has been further supported by the work of Edelman (2019) in the development of their annual Trust Barometer. They have found that between January and December 2018, the stock performance of 31 high-trust US companies outperformed their sector by an average of 5%.

Developing trustworthiness

The DARE model is a key way to develop trust and progress towards the benefits described above. By using DARE to build trust in others – and getting them to trust you – you will all share more confidential and personal information. This in turn leads to more connected relationships and the opportunity to challenge others and enhance their performance. Those around you will also have more certainty on how you are likely to behave, which enables you to have greater consistency of leadership. Your team will be more reliable and you will need to spend less time checking and following up. There will be a culture of support.

Life's lessons

Can you imagine a world where people have developed through all four stages of DARE? Where they have high levels of self-awareness, excellent skills at reading others and interpreting their behaviour accurately? Where they then use that knowledge for ethical purposes and the greater good of all?

For individuals in such a world, work is fulfilling, rewarding and enjoyable. They go to the office motivated and excited. They have great relationships with their colleagues. These work relationships are based on support and connection, as well as positive challenges. Their goals are achieved and they deliver results. Those who sit at the 'top table' positively influence others. Their teams are motivated and inspired to perform. As leaders who understand what drives others, they help their people find their purpose at work and play to their strengths. Their teams are proud to deliver and achieve their personal best. They feel fulfilled and energetic for the challenges ahead.

In fact, teams in this ideal world of DARE will be high-performing and deliver superior performance. Their members will understand each other's drivers and work highly effectively together. They will appreciate and value diversity – and the creativity and innovation that results from difference. People will feel part of something great and inclusive. Their brains in these circumstances will perform optimally to develop both the most creative and the most analytical solutions.

Relationships with family and friends will also be positive and uplifting. In the imaginary world of DARE, you will understand what people really need from you and how you can give them what they need in a way that 'lands with' them. You will develop greater intimacy by having a deeper connection. In turn this will lead to more mutual support and unsurpassed levels of trust and loyalty.

On planet DARE, life is in balance, while work and home are in harmony. Working hours are reasonable and there is plenty of time to enjoy with family and friends. Furthermore, when you are with family and friends, you are fully present with both mind and body. Whilst there are times when long working hours are inevitable, they are expected and not detrimental to your primary relationships at home (Figure 11.2).

Could this be our world? A world where people do not misinterpret the actions and words of others? For sure there will be evil people who use empathic influencing for their own gain and others' loss, but they will be in the minority. Remember, we demonise others based on our own self-talk rather than what they truly say and mean. Just imagine what would happen if we could be clearer on this!

Figure 11.2 Planet DARE.

If we all truly appreciated the impact of our actions and words on others, what that would mean in terms of crime? How could you hurt another if you really understood how that would feel to that person?

Today, we live in a world where people commit the most heinous of crimes. Innocent victims go about their business and are murdered in the name of ideology. If the perpetrators really understood and felt the pain and suffering of others, how could they commit acts of terror? Could they be part of any ideology that condoned such atrocities?

I believe that it is incumbent on all of us to understand the perspectives of others – and to use this skill to play our small part in building a better world.

At the time of writing this book, there is a lot of debate about two movements: #metoo and #timesup. The #metoo movement deals with sexual assault and harassment of women. Although it had been around for many years and was founded initially by Tarana Burke, it was in the aftermath of revelations about Harvey Weinstein's abuse of actress Alyssa Milano that thousands of women declared their own 'metoo' experiences. The 'timesup' movement is focused more on workplace equality and equal economic opportunities for women and people of colour.

If men, or indeed all people who have power over others, really understood how their actions impacted others, then there would be no need for these movements. If people in power could only apply cognitive, affective and somatic empathy, it would be difficult for them to perpetuate such actions. So often, those who offend (or merely give offence) have not thought through how it feels to be on the receiving end of their own behaviour.

One consequence of these movements is that men are worried about how to behave in the workplace. At one end of the scale, there is concern about the appropriateness of playful comments and banter. And at the other extreme, men are anxious about finding themselves alone with people of the opposite sex. Furthermore, both men and women are troubled by the potential sterility of a work environment, where after all 15% of people meet their partners.

However, by consciously employing DARE in these situations, you can avert concerns and promote positive, successful working relationships. The DARE model is incompatible with hurting and harassing others. If you really understand others, recognising who they are at level 3, and are alert to reading them and their reactions (both positive and negative), your actions at level 4 will be authentic, respectful and considerate.

Summary of key points

- Trust is at the heart of everything.
- High trust increases certainty in our brains.
- Trust triggers the release of oxytocin, a chemical that creates pro-social and positive feelings for others, thus promoting empathy.
- High-trust environments yield superior business performance and greater individual joy.
- The DARE model is a key way to develop trust.
- DARE leads to positive relationships in and out of work, as well as helping to create high-performing teams.
- DARE leads to a better balance between work and home life.
- Authentic leaders who DARE can have a significant impact on the world as a whole.

References

Covey, S. M. R. (2006). *The Speed of Trust*. London: Simon & Schuster.
Edelman. (2019). *Edelman Trust Barometer Executive Summary*. Accessed: January 24, 2019. www.Edelman.com.
Zak, P. J. (2012). *The Moral Molecule: The Source of Love and Prosperity*. New York: Dutton.
Zak, P. J. (2014). The Neuroscience of Trust. *People and Strategy*, vol. 37, no. 1, pp. 14–17.
Zak, P. J. (2017). The Neuroscience of Trust. *Harvard Business Review*, vol. 95 January–February.

Index